TESTIMONIES OF FORMER STUDENTS

"Every now and then God chooses to plant someone on our planet with an extra measure of anointing and insight. Without question, Dr. Thomson K. Mathew is one such person. I had the privilege of attending Dr. Mathew's lectures as a DMin student at India Bible College and Seminary. It provided me with much inspiration and added a real burden to emphasize disciple making and spiritual formation in my ministry. The fulfilment of the Great Commission is a core theme of Dr. Mathew's teaching. His instruction imparted knowledge and ignited a fire within all students to live out our faith with authenticity and purpose. Personally, I learned the importance of embodying the love and grace of Christ in pastoral care and spiritual formation.

"I can confidently testify that Dr. Mathew exhibited extraordinary teaching skills with conviction and Christian values. The concepts of disciple-making and kingdom citizenship challenged me to go beyond surface-level engagement with Scripture and, instead, to dive deep into the transformative power of God's Word. I have embedded the concepts from Dr. Mathew's teaching in my sermons. His passion for spreading the gospel inspired me to reinforce the truth that the duty of discipleship is every believer's business in my ministry in England and Northeast India. Also, I have incorporated this as a subject to orient the pastors working with me in Northeast India.

"I am profoundly grateful for Dr. Thomson Mathew's influence in my life and ministry. His willingness to share his wealth of experience and insight in this book is a testament to his heart for equipping and empowering believers to lead world-impacting lives. I am confident that his words will continue to inspire and transform countless lives just as they have mine."

—**Pastor James Chacko**, DMin (Cand.)
Senior Pastor, Hebron Pentecostal Assembly, United Kingdom
President, The Indian Pentecostal Church
of God, Meghalaya State, India

"Words cannot describe the depth of Dr. Thomson Mathew's indelible impact on my life—a relationship that started sixteen years ago. I was a doctor of ministry student at Oral Roberts University when we first met. His teaching, discipleship, and mentorship have profoundly shaped my roles as a father, college and seminary professor, Christian minister, disciple maker, and leadership consultant. His guidance has instilled in me a commitment to spiritual disciplines such as prayer and discernment—recognizing them as essential for spiritual growth and effective decision-making.

"Dr. Mathew's emphasis on leveraging spiritual principles from the life of Jesus and the apostles has equipped me with invaluable tools to navigate the complexities of human behavior and decision-making in ministry and academia. His influence continues to shape my professional endeavors and my ongoing journey with Christ, inspiring me to approach every aspect of ministry and education with humility, curiosity, and a steadfast commitment to truth.

"I enjoyed reading the draft of the manuscript titled *From Membership to Discipleship: The Path to Spiritual Formation and a World-Impacting Life.* I am confident this book will empower so many church leaders and their congregations by influencing them to adopt the life and ministry paradigm proposed in this book"

—**William Valmyr**, PhD, DMin
CEO, Transformational Leadership, LLC
Adjunct Professor, Southeastern University
Florida, USA

"Dr. Thomson K. Mathew is an exemplary figure in discipleship, spirituality, and global missions. As a local pastor in New Haven, chaplain at City of Faith Medical and Research Center in Tulsa, and professor at Oral Roberts University (ORU), he has provided a rich model of ministry through his extensive experience. While I was studying at ORU Seminary, he was one of my most memorable professors, offering not only instruction but also prayers and blessings as Jesus did when He sent out His disciples. I vividly remember Dr. Mathew laying hands on each student and praying for them and feeling the presence of God.

"I had the privilege to translate Dr. Thomson Mathew's book *Spiritual Identity and Spirit-Empowered Life* into Korean that provided me with much inspiration and practical help for my ministry in Korea. Currently working as a Korean language instructor for internationals, I conduct education and counseling ministry for professionals employed in major Korean companies. I have witnessed the crisis of identity experienced by individuals from various cultural backgrounds living in multicultural environments. Dr. Mathew's book on spiritual identity has been a great resource to me. This latest publication also contains precious truths about discipleship, spiritual formation, and global missions, which I believe will offer invaluable instruction to ministers and disciples worldwide."

—**Rev. Young K. Ju**, Chaplain
CLT Company
Seoul, Republic of Korea

Also by Thomson K. Mathew

Ministry between Miracles

Prayer, Medicine, and Healing

A Seminary Dean's Experiment with Servant Leadership

Spiritual Identity and Spirit-Empowered Life

Spiritual Identity and Spirit-Empowered Life Leader's Guide

Spirit-Led Ministry in the Twenty-First Century

What Will Your Tombstone Say?

Ministry Research Simplified

[ALL AVAILABLE ON AMAZON]

FROM MEMBERSHIP TO DISCIPLESHIP

FROM MEMBERSHIP TO DISCIPLESHIP

The Path to Spiritual Formation
And a World-Impacting Life

THOMSON K. MATHEW

From Membership to Discipleship: The Path to Spiritual Formation and a World-Impacting Life

Published by:
GOODNEWS BOOKS
Kottayam, Kerala 686 004, India

Global version published independently in the United States.

Paperback ISBN: 978-1-7379780-2-2
Ebook ISBN: 978-1-7379780-5-3

Cover and interior design: Creative Publishing Book Design
Cover photo: Image licensed by Shutterstock

To Fiju, Amy, and Jamie who have decided
to take up the cross and follow Jesus,
to Philip and Joseph who just began their journey of faith,
to siblings who are sojourners, and
to grandparents and parents who have gone before us!

Thomson K. and Molly Mathew

CONTENTS

FOREWORD

Jesus commissioned His disciples before His ascension, "Go therefore and make disciples of all the nations, baptizing them in the name of the Father and of the Son and of the Holy Spirit, teaching them to observe all things that I have commanded you." Jesus assured His disciples that all authority had been given to Him in heaven and on earth and that He would be with them (Matt. 28:18–20). These verses encapsulate the essence of Thomson K. Mathew's book *From Membership to Discipleship: The Path to Spiritual Formation and a World-Impacting Life.* In Mathew's book Christians and churches are encouraged to embrace Jesus' commission to make disciples.

When Jesus chose His twelve disciples to walk with Him during His three years of active ministry while on earth, He said, "Follow me, and I will make you fishers of men" (Matt. 4:19). They followed Him as He modeled for them what it meant to be a disciple. He took them with Him as He went about all of Galilee, "teaching in their synagogues, preaching the gospel of the kingdom, and healing all kinds of sickness and all kinds of disease among the people" (Matt. 4:23; see also Matt. 9:35). Just prior to His ascension, Jesus confirmed with His disciples that He had fulfilled what was written about Him "in the Law of Moses and the Prophets and the Psalms" (Luke 24:44) while He was with them. Moreover, "He opened their understanding, that they might comprehend the Scriptures" (v. 45).

What a privilege Jesus' disciples had! Today, however, we are privileged to have the Holy Spirit who opens our understanding of the Scriptures and provides guidance (John 14:25–26). We also have leaders, mentors, and insightful books, such as Mathew's book, as we are on our life's journey to become like Jesus and, in turn, disciple others. Paul wrote, "And we all, who with unveiled faces contemplate the Lord's glory, are being transformed into his image with ever-increasing glory, which comes from the Lord, who is the Spirit" (2 Cor. 3:18 NIV). May we be able to share with our disciples as Paul did, "Follow my example, as I follow the example of Christ" (1 Cor. 11:1 NIV).

Mathew's book provides a well-defined and well-researched path for churches, Christian discipleship organizations, and Christians. Mathew draws from his own experience and expertise in the field of discipleship, spiritual growth, and spiritual formation, as well as from other experts in related fields who underscore and substantiate the premise of his book.

Mathew's book is a timely treatise for churches, Christians, and church leaders. He supplies the reader with knowledge, inspiration, resources, and examples for defining this pathway from membership to discipleship that leads to spiritual growth and formation for Christians and the development of a new ministry paradigm for churches.

Mathew is an outstanding example of a man of God who is successfully fulfilling God's call and purpose for his life. He is an excellent communicator of sound biblical, theological, and practical skills in his teachings and writings. He has extensive experience as a pastor, chaplain, seminary professor of pastoral care, and former dean of the Oral Roberts University College of Theology and Ministry, a well-known pentecostal-charismatic seminary. As the former associate dean of the ORU Seminary, I personally observed his compassion, pastoral care, and discipling skills with students, faculty, administration, and Christian leaders here in the United States and in other countries.

Mathew is a devoted husband, father, grandfather, colleague, and my friend for twenty-five years. He is an author, conference speaker, preacher, and educator at home and abroad. With his wealth of knowledge and experience, Mathew is well qualified to write his book *From Membership to Discipleship: The Path to Spiritual Formation and a World-Impacting Life.* Moreover, he is well versed in the state of churches today, both at home and in countries around the world. As you read Mathew's book, may you be challenged and inspired to follow Jesus and fulfill His Great Commission (Matt. 28:18–20).

Cheryl L. Iverson, PhD
Professor Emeritus and Former Associate Dean
College of Theology and Ministry
Oral Roberts University

DEFINITIONS

Discipleship

1. Discipleship is a journey that leads to spiritual growth and life transformation.
2. Discipleship is the exercise of the kingdom lifestyle here and now.
3. Discipleship is a journey of faith that leads to heaven.
4. Discipleship is the journey from being the image of God to becoming the likeness of Christ.

Spiritual Growth or Spiritual Development or Faith Development

1. Spiritual growth is spiritual development in three dimensions: (1) the cognitive (thinking) aspect of faith, (2) the affective dimension that deals with affections and commitment, and (3) the behavioral aspects of faith. It manifests in all three dimensions of our personality: body, mind, and spirit.

2. Spiritual growth involves both knowing faith (doctrine), feeling faith (emotions and values), and living faith (lifestyle).

Spiritual Formation

1. Spiritual formation is a lifelong journey in pursuit of being conformed to the image of Jesus Christ. It is a lifelong process of sanctification involving learning and change that is measured in terms of Christlikeness in the believer.
2. Spiritual formation is more than increased biblical knowledge or cognitive development in spirituality. It is a divine work of grace involving the Word of God, the Spirit of Christ, and the community of faith that transforms and empowers an individual to live as a fruit-bearing follower of Jesus. This transformation of life represents not just conforming responses to external pressures, but decisions, choices, and actions that are governed by the internal motivations of a Spirit-led person.

INTRODUCTION

As a pastor, chaplain, seminary dean, and frequent listener to pastors in several nations, I have concluded the global church has lost its way regarding its main business, which is to make disciples (not adherents). Jesus gave His followers only one assignment: "Go therefore and make disciples of all the nations" (Matt. 28:19). Generally speaking, the church across the world gives lip service to the Great Commission, but its budgets and activities do not support this mission as a priority. Of course, we say the ultimate purpose of the church is to make disciples, but our major investments of time, talent, and treasure are made in the maintenance of membership, not in discipleship or disciple making.

I have heard it said that companies that forget their main business always fail. For instance, I was told the railroad business in the United States failed when the airlines prospered because the railroad leaders forgot they were in the transportation business, not just moving goods from point A to point B. Likewise, telephone companies are not in the phone manufacturing business; they are in the business of communication. The church's main business is not membership maintenance or real estate investment. Its main business is making disciples who grow spiritually, live as fully devoted followers of Jesus, and impact the world.

I have wondered what would happen if churches were accredited like educational institutions. As the dean of the Oral Roberts University College of Theology and Ministry (ORUCTM), I was given the duty to preserve the high-level accreditation that was granted to the Oral Roberts University Seminary by the Association of Theological Schools in the United States and Canada (ATS). ATS is considered the gold standard of graduate theological education in the world. This meant I was constantly watching the quality of theological education that was taking place under my supervision. As required for all accredited seminaries, ATS sends a site visit team consisting of deans and professors from peer institutions to campuses around the two countries. They examine everything that happens, from recruitment of students to their graduation, in a step-by-step fashion. That meant they looked at the mission of the school, the objectives of the degree programs, the preparedness and work of the faculty, the adequacy of the facilities and finances, student experiences, student learning assessments, the graduation rate, etc. All evaluative questions of the site visit team are based on what the school claims to be its institutional mission.

Seminaries scheduled for a site visit start their self-examination about eighteen months prior to the visit and look at all the above areas in an objective way, with full document review, and prepare a detailed self-study report. Seminaries will list their self-discovered strengths and their weaknesses in these reports and present realistic plans to improve those weaknesses. The visiting team will examine everything thoroughly and recommend either renewal of accreditation with commendations or list the conditions needing remedy. Depending on the degree of violations or weaknesses, written explanations are required and/or more frequent visits are imposed. Repeated violations of serious matters can result in a suspension of accreditation. I was blessed with an outstanding faculty, hardworking staff, and great support from the university president and the board of trustees. ATS renewed our accreditation for ten years, the maximum period allowed, each time we were evaluated during my tenure.

Without getting into the contemporary controversies about freedom of religion and government interventions (ATS is not a government agency but operates with accountability to the US Department of Education), I wonder how most churches would fare if someone with authority over them put them through this type of rigorous review based on the biblical mission of all churches. How many churches would pass such a test? Why do we tolerate the current status of discipleship and spiritual formation within our local congregations? When will we insist on implementing the real mission of the church—the Great Commission—to be the primary mission of the church and hold the churches accountable to that mission?

Dear pastor, leader, or church member: Fully devoted followers of Jesus must do more than attend worship services and pay tithes. They also need to do more than attend the so-called care groups that normally are poorly run didactic groups led by well-meaning people who are trained neither in caring nor in teaching. This should change.

No, I am not trying to make the pastors' life more miserable. I know that the Covid pandemic was tough on pastors and churches. I have seen the Barna report and am aware of the rate of burnout among pastors and the percentage of preachers who are quitting the business.[1] But could it be that what is burning them out is the missing discipleship work itself? Under the pressure of the secular corporate model of evaluations—considering only the church's budget, buildings, and bodies in seats, and being compared unfairly to media-savvy social media star pastors with large numbers of friends and likes—are the hardworking godly pastors being mistreated by the churches?

I know of a social media personality pastor of a megachurch in the Southeast United States. One of his volunteer care group leaders had to get himself ordained online by a questionable organization to conduct the wedding of a church member in his care group because the star pastor does not do such things for the members in his church, and he has no staff associates assigned to offer pastoral counseling or conduct weddings for tithe-paying members of his congregation. One can imagine the number of disciples produced in this church! Thankfully, this pastor does not represent most pastors, who are self-giving servants of God, but he is a symptom of our current situation in the global church. How sad!

I don't expect pastors of larger or megachurches to care for everyone or disciple everyone in their congregations personally, but the responsibility is still theirs to implement something that meets the care needs of the congregation and to accomplish the true mission of the church: disciple making. This is doable. I know of large and small congregations across the world where this does happen, but they are few.

The church can be more than a social club. The church can do more than offer public worship opportunities. The church can do more than offer traditional Sunday schools where the focus is only on the transfer of biblical information. The church can do more than pacify people whom the apostle Paul calls natural or carnal. The church can do more than produce what Ed Stetzer calls "cultural Christians" and "congregational Christians."[2] Indeed, the church can make disciples of Jesus, help them to grow spiritually, become transformed in the process, and become disciple makers and kingdom citizens who will discern and follow God's call on their lives. The church can truly help believers to grow in grace and in the knowledge of our Lord and Savior Jesus Christ and live as fully devoted followers of Jesus.

Let me share with you one example. A few years ago, I met a young evangelist in India at the conclusion of my father's funeral service. My father was the pastor of a South Indian congregation for three decades while he served as a district supervisor in his denomination. The young minister wanted to express his gratitude for my father's ministry in that part of the world and particularly the impact he had on him personally. He said, "When I first met your father, I met him as his shoe repairman. He became a spiritual father and mentor to me. Today I serve as a minister because of his investment in my life." Somehow, my father turned his shoe repairman into a preacher of the gospel through discipleship and mentoring. Disciple making is still a possibility in the twenty-first century.

This book is my humble contribution to address this concern for discipleship. With the premise that pastors and churches can change, I begin the first chapter of this book with a comprehensive look at discipleship as it relates to the kingdom of God. Chapter 2 presents an in-depth examination of transformational discipleship. I have attempted to present some of the best thinkers on this topic in this chapter. Chapter 3 deals with spiritual growth and the stages of spiritual development based on different theories and perspectives. I present concepts from important studies of human development and faith development in this chapter. The next two chapters deal with the idea of spiritual formation as sanctification and nonlegalistic spirituality. I present a wholistic understanding of spiritual formation and progressive sanctification in chapter 4, presenting insights from Henri Nouwen, Dallas Willard, and others. I deal with the problem of legalism and the opposite—hypergrace theology—in chapter 5 and present a healthy nonlegalistic and liberating biblical spirituality. Here again, I am indebted to the experts in the field who have inspired me.

Chapter 6 examines the concept of God's call to discipleship that may lead to vocational ministry. This chapter focuses on disciple making and the potential of mature disciples considering full-time Christian ministry as a vocation. The cost of discipleship as suffering is the theme of chapter 7. The apostle Paul's experiences and theological views of suffering are included in this chapter, along with perspectives from godly thinkers such as Dietrich Bonhoeffer, E. Stanley Jones, and C. S. Lewis.

Chapter 8 is devoted to encouraging individuals who sense a call to vocational ministry to seek confirmation of their call, prepare to embark on it, and to develop a strong ministerial identity. Disciple making is not just education, although it involves teaching and learning. Chapter 9 presents discipling as adult education based on the methods Jesus, the model disciple maker, used to teach and form His disciples. Here again I present research from the field of adult education (andragogy) in nontechnical language. The last chapter includes information to help pastors to move discipleship to the center of their ministries in their churches and to fulfill the Great Commission by developing contextually appropriate plans to make disciples and disciple makers.

I have written about certain aspects of discipleship in some of my previous books and articles. I have adapted relevant portions from some of these writings to present a comprehensive look at this vital topic in this book. I trust my readers will benefit from the addition of these elements in this book.

As an academic dean, I invited experts in the ministry of discipleship to teach at ORU Seminary as adjunct professors. I recall inviting Bill Hull, author of the classic book *The Disciple-Making Pastor*, to teach a course. The students were greatly impacted by his teaching on discipleship. Later I invited Dr. John Thannickal, founder of New Life Ashram and New Life College in Bangalore, to teach on discipleship and global mission. His students were so touched and motivated by his life and teaching that I invited him to teach the course annually as a visiting professor. I am afraid typical seminaries are emphasizing preaching, pastoral care, counseling, etc., but not training disciple makers. This may be a factor in the current situation in the churches. Recently, I taught a DMin course titled Discipleship, Spiritual Formation, and Ministry at the India Bible College and Seminary in Kerala, India. Students who attended this course from India, the Middle East, and England reported on their efforts to implement discipleship ministries at their churches. They also encouraged me to publish some of what they heard in my class presentations. I am grateful to them for their encouragement, which resulted in this book.

I am grateful to my wife, Molly; my daughters, Amy and Jamie; Amy's husband, Fiju; and my grandsons, Philip and Joseph, who are all a constant encouragement to me. I am also grateful to Dr. Cheryl Iverson, my longtime colleague, professor emeritus, and former associate dean of ORU College of Theology and Ministry, who wrote a thoughtful and kind foreword, and to editor in chief C. V. Mathew (no relation) of Goodnews Books.

I hope pastors, spiritual leaders, and church members who are serious about their faith will find this book helpful and encouraging. If one congregation changes its emphasis to disciple making, and if one pastor is moved by this challenge, and if one believer is inspired to follow Jesus as a fully devoted follower, I will be more than gratified.

Wishing my readers all God's best,

Thomson K. Mathew, DMin, EdD
Professor Emeritus and Former Dean
College of Theology and Ministry
Oral Roberts University

CHAPTER 1

THE KINGDOM OF GOD AND DISCIPLESHIP

He sent them to preach the kingdom of God and to heal the sick. (Luke 9:2)

It has been widely recognized there is not much difference between the lifestyles of Americans who claim to be Christians and those who do not. Researcher George Barna discovered that only 9 percent of born-again adults have a biblical worldview and started sounding the alarm regarding the worsening spiritual condition of American Christians more than a decade ago. In a later study he presented more concerning statistics. Only 20 percent of all Christian adults were involved in one of the four discipleship activities: (1) Sunday school or fellowship group (43 percent), (2) spiritual mentoring (17 percent), (3) study the Bible in a group setting (33 percent), and (4) reading or discussing a Christian book (25 percent).[3] Only 19 percent of self-identified Christians made daily Scripture reading a habit.[4] Barna discovered that most born-again Christians base their moral choices on their feelings instead of the Word of God, and he concluded, "most Americans who confess their sins to God and ask Christ to be their Savior live almost indistinguishable from the unrepentant sinners, and their lives bear little, if any fruit, for the Kingdom of God."[5]

Barna's discovery was consistent with the self-study done by Willow Creek Church in South Barrington, Illinois, where Bill Hybels was the senior pastor. Willow Creek pastors were shocked to find that their "highly successful" ministries and programs, which were promoted widely as effective disciple makers, were not effective at all.[6] This sobering discovery caused them to make significant changes to their ministries.

Recent studies show that things are not getting better spiritually in the post-Covid church. While 28 percent of Christians claim to belong to a discipleship community, only 5 percent are discipling others, and 39 percent have nothing to do with discipleship.[7] Additionally, the number of American adults describing themselves religiously as "nones" is shockingly high. According to the Pew Research Center, between 2007 and 2023, this group grew from 16 percent to 28 percent. For two years during this period, the rate of nones reached 29 percent (2021) and 31 percent (2022).[8] The newly coined term "Exvangelicals" is an indicator of the current spiritual condition of the evangelical churches in America. What is becoming evident is that the Bible-believing, conversion-preaching evangelical churches and tongue-speaking, miracle-believing pentecostal and charismatic congregations are not investing much in discipleship, disciple making, and the spiritual formation of their members.

Greg Ogden, former professor at Fuller Theological Seminary, presented seven reasons for the poor state of discipleship today: (1) passive ministers, (2) a casual Christian life, (3) faith considered a private matter, (4) yielding to cultural pressures, (5) optional church commitment, (6) biblical illiteracy, and (7) a lack of witnessing.[9] I believe Ogden identified the practical reasons for the current situation, but I am convinced there is something more fundamental behind this disaster. I concluded, fundamentally, modern Christians lack a true understanding of the concept of the kingdom of God that Jesus taught, the lifestyle it requires, and the invitation they received to embody it. Let us begin with a review of Jesus' teachings about the kingdom of God.

The Kingdom of God

John the Baptist came preaching the kingdom of God, and he was beheaded. Jesus picked up the message, saying, "Repent, for the kingdom of God is at hand," and He was crucified. His disciples continued the message, and they also paid with their lives.

The declaration of the coming kingdom of God began with a call to repentance. The world never liked such a call, but kingdom life begins with repentance. In the Gospels, *repent* is not a request; it is a command. Jesus told Zacchaeus, "Come down!" and to Matthew, He said, "Follow me." To the rich young ruler Jesus said, "Sell your possessions and give to the poor." These were not meant as requests; they were commands. The call to repentance is a command.

We are all familiar with the idea of naturalization, the process through which an immigrant becomes a citizen. Unfortunately, no one is naturalized into the kingdom of God; one must be "born again." Two kingdoms exist—the kingdom of darkness and the kingdom of light—and you must die in one to enter the other. More specifically, you must die in one to be born into the other. The kingdom of God is a kingdom of light and a kingdom of life. As we enter the kingdom of life, we pass from death to life.

The kingdom of God is a divine concept. It is not meat or drink; it has to do with righteousness, peace, and joy in the Holy Spirit (Rom. 14:17). It is the sphere of the rule and reign of God.

It appears there are four dimensions of the kingdom of God that inform us about the requirements of a kingdom lifestyle on planet Earth. These are listed as

1. The concept of time in the kingdom of God
2. The values of the kingdom of God
3. The priorities of the kingdom of God
4. The mysteries of the kingdom of God

Let us examine these briefly.

Time in the Kingdom of God

According to the Word of God, the kingdom of God has arrived; His kingdom arrived when Jesus came into the world and announced, "The kingdom of God is at hand." The kingdom of God involves the past, the present, and the future. In terms of the past, the kingdom has come (Matt. 3:2). Concerning the present, the kingdom of God is here now; it is in our midst, manifesting the power of the Holy

Spirit (Luke 17:21). With respect to the future, the kingdom of God is yet coming (Matt. 6:10). The cosmic fullness of the kingdom of God is yet to come.

So we live now between the kingdom come and the kingdom coming. We live by faith and enjoy many benefits of the kingdom of God now. Salvation, healing, signs and wonders, and the gifts of the Spirit are current benefits of the kingdom of God. And yet there is a level of kingdom fullness we have not seen so far. For instance, not all our prayers are answered now. Not all suffering is removed yet. The innocent still suffer. The sick are not all healed. Loved ones die. Persecution goes on. But the fullness of God's kingdom will come, Jesus promised. Until then, knowing the suffering of this present time is not worthy to be compared with the glory that will be revealed in us (Rom. 8:18), we continue to pray, "Father, thy kingdom come!" We know that when that day comes God will wipe away all our tears (Isa. 25:8).

So how shall we live between the kingdom come and the kingdom coming? The answer is simple: We shall live by faith in the Son of God who loved us and gave Himself for us (Gal. 2:20). We shall live a kingdom lifestyle in this world. What does a kingdom lifestyle look like? Before we can answer that question, we must consider the values, priorities, and mysteries of the kingdom of God.

Values of the Kingdom of God

The values of the kingdom of God are upside down. For instance, in God's kingdom, giving is the way to receiving: "Give, and it will be given to you. A good measure, pressed down, shaken together and running over, will be poured into your lap. For with the measure you use, it will be measured to you" (Luke 6:38 NIV). In the kingdom of God, serving is the way to lead, because the last shall be the first (Mark 10:31) and dying is the way to live: "Whoever wants to be my disciple must deny themselves and take up their cross and follow me. For whoever wants to save their life will lose it, but whoever loses their life for me and for the gospel will save it" (Mark 8:34–35 NIV).

These are not just abstract theoretical positions for a citizen of the kingdom of God. These are actual values we are expected to live by. There is no way to live this way without a cost. I have seen many young people and new believers shocked to find out they lost friends or jobs because of the values of the kingdom of God they adopted. I know people who were denied professional advancement because they refused to compromise their kingdom convictions. Some faced discrimination. Others faced ridicule. I remember my parents and grandparents in India, taking newly converted Christians into their homes who were disowned by their loved ones and disinherited by their families because they responded to the Lord's invitation to join His kingdom. Yes, there is a price to pay, but I have also seen the Lord opening wider doors and incredible opportunities to many who remained faithful. And according to the Word of God, God will remember and reward the others who have not received an immediate reward: "And everyone who left houses or brothers or sisters or father or mother or wife or children or lands, for My name's sake, shall receive a hundredfold, and inherit eternal life" (Matt. 19:29).

Priorities of the Kingdom of God

The priorities of the kingdom of God are also unlike the world's. In the kingdom, formation is more important than information, and unconditional love is a priority. The kingdom is governed by the principles of *agape* (unconditional love). This love goes beyond neighborly love or brotherly love and is more like trinity love. What does trinity love look like? According to Juan Carlos Ortiz, author of the well-known book *Disciple,*[10] it looks like mashed potatoes. You can claim unity just by being together with others, like potatoes in a sack. They can sit in the bag and sing about unity, saying, "We are in the same bag, and we have the same brand name." They could also say, "I am a big potato and you are a small potato," or, "Look at me, I'm a white potato and you're a brown potato." Often, this is the only kind of unity that we have in our churches. But if you take the potatoes out of the bag, peel them, cut them into pieces, put them in a pot, and boil them to make mashed potatoes, something new happens to these potatoes. They are the same potatoes, but now no one can distinguish the big potato from the small potato. One cannot tell the difference between the white potato and the brown potato because they have become one. According to Ortiz, this kind of love represents trinity love, which allows us to sing, "We are one in the Spirit; we are one in the Lord." The authentic Christian life is a life that gives priority to love and unity.

Most of us are not used to agape love, because it is unconditional and divine in nature. We have become accustomed to conditional love, which I call "if" or "because of" love. God presents us with "in spite of" love, and He desires we be filled with this love: "But God demonstrates His own love toward us, in that while we were still sinners, Christ died for us" (Rom. 5:8).

Genuine relationships are a priority in the kingdom of God. Kingdom relationships function like the various parts of the human body; all are members of one body, uniting each other, supporting each other, passing along nourishment to each other, and making room for each other. "For as we have many members in one body, but all the members do not have the same function, so we, being many, are one body in Christ, and individually members of one another" (Rom. 12:4–5). In the kingdom, we are not in competition with one another, and we don't attack each other. We support and nurture one another. Look at the biblical metaphors for the church: body of Christ, building made with living stones, household of faith, family of God, and communion of saints. All indicate intimate relationships. All imply strong connections and purposeful unity.

Worship also is a priority in the kingdom of God. Worship may be called the language of the kingdom of God. So is preaching. Kingdom citizens are called to bear witness to the King. They are to preach that He is Savior, Healer, Lord, and King.

Mysteries of the Kingdom of God

According to the parables of Jesus, the kingdom of God involves certain mysteries. First, everything about the kingdom is not visible.

It is like salt, not visible, but very influential and discernable: "You are the salt of the earth. But if the salt loses its saltiness, how can it be made salty again? It is no longer good for anything, except to be thrown out and trampled underfoot" (Matt. 5:13 NIV).

The kingdom of God is like invisible yeast that causes the dough to rise and expand: "It is like yeast that a woman took and mixed into about sixty pounds of flour until it worked all through the dough" (Luke 13:21 NIV).

Good and bad coexist in the kingdom of God. The wheat and the tares grow together for a season, but a separation will come (Matt. 13:24–29). Good fish and bad fish will coexist in the net for a while, but a sorting will come (Matt. 13:47–49). This is a mystery.

Another mystery is that the beauty of the kingdom of God is not visible on the outside. It does not appear attractive to everyone. Like the tabernacle in the wilderness that hosted the presence of God, the outside of the kingdom of God is unattractive. But there are those who will discover the beauty and value of the kingdom and belong to it at any cost. Like a man who finds unexpected treasure in a land and sells everything he has to buy it, or a merchant who finds a pearl of great price and sells everything he has to own it, there are those who will give up everything for the kingdom of God (Matt. 13:44–45). While his neighbors see only dirt, the man who gives up everything knows it contains a great treasure. The merchant is the only one who recognizes the value of the pearl while others are surprised by the transaction. The kingdom of God is a mystery. What is the treasure in the kingdom of God? What is the pearl of great price? In the final analysis, the treasure is Jesus. He is the pearl of great price. Anyone who finds Him finds everything for life and eternal life. This is a great mystery.

Kingdom Lifestyle

So what is the kingdom's lifestyle? It is a life of discipleship, and it involves living in a different time frame. You live your life in everyday calendar time (*chronos*), but you are attuned to God's fullness of time (*kairos*). You live here and now, but your frame of reference is something beyond here and now. You accept Jesus Christ not just as your savior and healer, but as your lord and master. You live as if you have traded everything for Him. That means you have spiritually traded your degree, home, car, spouse, kids, money, friends, and all for Him. You may still formally possess all of these things, but they are no longer yours in your spirit or attitude. They belong to Jesus.

As a requirement of this lifestyle of discipleship, you adopt kingdom values for yourself. You begin to give as if it is the very act of receiving. You die daily, having been beckoned to come and die with Jesus, as Dietrich Bonhoeffer said. You serve others as if your life depends on it, adopting a lifestyle of servant leadership.

Your priorities also change as you live as a disciple of Jesus. You seek the kingdom of God first, knowing that everything you need will be given to you (Matt. 6:33). You live a life of repentance, loving others, worshipping God, and bearing witness to the King of glory.

You depend on God to live out the mystery of the kingdom of God in your time and place. You will put your hands to the plow as Jesus said and will not look back (Luke 9:62). Your lips will carry the words of the old hymn: "I have decided to follow Jesus. No turning back." And you will preach, teach, bear witness, and minister healing as the Lord gives you opportunities.

Contemporary Situation

Disciples of Jesus are citizens of the kingdom of God. Discipleship is the exercise of the kingdom lifestyle here and now. Unfortunately, contemporary Christians are grossly missing the mark in this regard. There seems to be three types of Christians in the world. Ed Stetzer names them cultural Christians, congregational Christians, and committed Christians. Each congregation seems to have a general constituency or parish, a worshipping congregation, and a group of committed Christians in a decreasing order of size.

Stetzer says that cultural Christianity is closer to deism than Christian faith. It affirms the faith without living it and believes in the dogma without practicing it. Congregational Christianity is not much better, as it allows one to belong to a community without necessarily supporting it, making one a spectator rather than a participant. True discipleship of committed Christians must be intentional, according to Stetzer, engaging the Bible, involving small groups, and focused on spiritual growth.

Many seem to be happy to have church membership rather than Christian discipleship. They prefer to be fans of Jesus rather than friends. The lack of discipleship among Christians has a significant impact on the nation, particularly in business, education, and politics. Civil religion and cultural Christianity cannot transform a community or nation. Religion manipulated by clever politicians for their own purposes cannot impact the world for God or influence communities with the principles of the kingdom of God. A culture of life and concern for ethics stem from true Christianity and are nurtured by costly discipleship. Cultural Christians who conveniently claim the Judeo-Christian heritage cannot transform a nation; they can only create a form of godliness without the power thereof (2 Tim. 3:5). It takes people who have counted the cost of discipleship and have decided to be fully devoted followers of Jesus to impact the world for God's purposes.

Churches must go back to Christ's mandate: "Therefore go and make disciples of all nations, baptizing them in the name of the Father and of the Son and of the Holy Spirit, and teaching them to obey everything I have commanded you" (Matt. 28:19–20 NIV). God's will is that Christ be formed in us. The apostle Paul considered this extremely painful to accomplish and expressed this sentiment to the Galatian believers: "My dear children, for whom I am again in the pains of childbirth until Christ is formed in you" (Gal. 4:19 NIV).

LeRoy Eims,[11] the well-known author on evangelism and discipleship, was right. A church that does not produce disciples is like a shoe factory that is running round the clock but does not produce any shoes! We have too many of these in the world.

Discipleship has to do with our relationship with Christ. It boils down to our proximity to Him or distance from Him. We can evaluate our relationship with the Lord in terms of biblical images. For instance, we can ask ourselves the following questions: Do I belong to the five thousand who enjoyed the bread and the fish or among the 120 who waited in the Upper Room? Am I among the seventy who were sent out to evangelize or among the twelve who were called to follow Jesus? Am I one of the three—Peter, James, and John—who accompanied Jesus to the Mount of Transfiguration? Or am I like John, who stood alone by the cross on that dreadful Friday? These are sobering thoughts.

The Lordship of Jesus

Disciples live under the lordship of Jesus. He is not just their savior or healer; He becomes the Lord of their life. Disciples live under the authority of Jesus, acknowledging that He holds all authority. The gospel of Luke testifies to the authority of Jesus in all areas of human life. Luke 8 gives a synopsis of this truth by illustrating Jesus' authority over (1) natural forces, (2) demonic power, (3) sicknesses, and (4) death.

Authority over Nature

While Jesus and the disciples were sailing across the Sea of Galilee, Jesus fell asleep. A great storm arose, which put all of them in grave danger, so the disciples cried out to Jesus and woke Him up. He rebuked the wind and the waves, and the wind and waves obeyed Him. Luke testifies of Jesus' authority over natural forces, which included stormy seas!

Authority over Demons

Luke then reports the healing of a demon-possessed man in the region of the Gadarenes. This man was living in the tombs, naked and deranged, but when he met Jesus, he fell at His feet: "Jesus asked him, 'What is your name?' 'Legion,' he replied, because many demons had gone into him. And they begged Jesus repeatedly not to order them to go into the Abyss" (Luke 8:30–31 NIV). Jesus gave the demons permission to go into a herd of pigs. The herd rushed into the lake and drowned, but the man who was set free sat at the feet of Jesus "dressed and in his right mind" (v. 35). According to Luke, Jesus has authority over demonic forces. They tremble at His presence and obey Him.

Authority over Sicknesses

Luke reports that upon Jesus' return from the region of the Gadarenes, a great crowd greeted Him and almost crushed Him. A particular woman in that crowd had been suffering from chronic bleeding for twelve years. Physicians could not heal her, and she was desperate. As this nameless woman came up behind Jesus and touched the edge of His garment, she was instantly healed. "Who touched me?" Jesus asked. "Someone touched me; I know that power has gone out of me," He added (Luke 8:45–46 NIV). The woman came forward, fell at His feet, and gave her testimony. "Daughter, your faith has healed you. Go in peace" (v. 48 NIV). In this passage, Luke shows that Jesus has authority over sicknesses and even over incurable diseases.

Authority over Death

Luke 8 concludes with the story of Jesus' raising the daughter of a man named Jairus, a synagogue ruler. While Jesus was ministering to the woman in the crowd who had just been healed, word came to Jairus that his beloved daughter was dead. Jesus said to Jairus, "Don't be afraid; just believe, and she will be healed" (v. 50 NIV). Jesus accompanied Jairus to his house and raised the twelve-year-old girl from the dead. "Her spirit returned, and at once she stood up" (v. 55 NIV). In this account, Luke presents the evidence for Jesus' ultimate authority, which extends even over the last enemy, death.

Matthew concluded his gospel with the words of Jesus: "All authority in heaven and on earth has been given to me. Therefore go and make disciples of all nations, baptizing them in the name of the Father and of the Son and of the Holy Spirit, and teaching them to obey everything I have commanded you. And surely I am with you always, to the very end of the age" (28:18–20 NIV). Jesus has all authority and He has given it to His disciples who are called to represent Him and His kingdom in this world. A true disciple accepts Jesus' authority over his own life and ministers to others in the authority given to him by Jesus. Discipleship involves both living under authority and exercising appropriate authority.

The mandate remains the same: the followers of Jesus are to make disciples of all ethnic groups (the word translated as "nations" is *ethnos* in Greek, Matt. 28:19). God's will is that the whole world would be saved through faith is Jesus Christ and that Christ be "formed in" each believer (Gal. 4:19 NIV). The ultimate purpose of this process is spiritual formation of every believer: "For whom He foreknew, He also predestined to be conformed to the image of His Son, that He might be the firstborn among many brethren" (Rom. 8:29).

Defining Discipleship

Who is a disciple? The Bible defines the disciple of Jesus as a learner and follower. As learners, they must develop character (Gal. 5:22–23), convictions (Heb. 11:24–25), and skills (Mark 7:37). This learning process is expected to be a formational experience that results in the development of a Christ-centered worldview and an eternal perspective on life in the believer.

Disciples must be faithful followers of Jesus. They must be willing to follow Jesus at any cost: "'Come, follow me,' Jesus said, 'and I will send you out to fish for people'" (Matt. 4:19 NIV). Luke reports: "No one who puts a hand to the plow and looks back is fit for service in the kingdom of God" (Luke 9:62 NIV). Disciples must follow the example of others who are faithful disciples; Paul said, "Follow my example, as I follow the example of Christ" (1 Cor. 11:1 NIV).

There is an action dimension to discipleship. Theologians call this praxis. The disciples must put into practice what they learn from their master. This will involve bearing witness to Christ in whatever means possible, such as preaching, teaching, or healing. Listen to Paul's advice: "Whatever you have learned or received or heard from me, or seen in me—put it into practice. And the God of peace will be with you" (Phil. 4:9 NIV). In this sense, disciples are apprentices of Christ.

The Bible gives a clear description of the character requirements of disciples. They must abide in Christ (John 15:7), bear fruit (v. 8), love Christ and others (Luke 14:26; John 13:34–35), and deny themselves (Luke 14:8–11). True disciples are cross bearers: "Then he said to them all: 'Whoever wants to be my disciple must deny themselves and take up their cross daily and follow me'" (Luke 9:23 NIV).

We must remember that until we were called Christians for the first time in Antioch, we were called disciples. Disciples are followers and learners (Luke 6:40). We follow Jesus and learn from Him. We learn character (Gal. 5:22–23), convictions (Heb. 11:24–25), skills (Mark 7:37), and perspective (Rom. 12:1–2) from Christ and His Word. We are apprentices who imitate the master and gain skills. Christ has called us (Matt. 4:19) and we have responded. There is no turning back (Luke 9:62).

As disciples, we abide in Jesus the vine (John 15:5–6) and bear fruit (John 15:7–8). We love Christ (Luke 14:26) and are willing to deny ourselves (Luke 14:11) and carry our cross (Luke 9:23; 14:27). We love others (John 13:34–35) and are committed to serve them in the name of Christ (Matt. 10:25; 25:40).

Discipleship is a formational journey, and it is transformational in effect. God's grace not only accepts and saves us, but it also transforms us. Discipleship moves people from decision (for Christ) to true conversion, and from conversion to sanctification. Disciples of Christ take the apostle's exhortation seriously: "Do not conform to the pattern of this world, but be transformed by the renewing of your mind. Then you will be able to test and approve what God's will is—his good, pleasing and perfect will" (Rom. 12:2 NIV).

True formation happens within a community, and it involves one's body, mind, spirit, and relationships. Paul's words summarize this process: "May God himself, the God of peace, sanctify you through and through. May your whole spirit, soul and body be kept blameless at the coming of our

Lord Jesus Christ" (1 Thess. 5:23 NIV). The Word of God, the Spirit of Christ, and the community of faith are involved in this journey of faith.

The Church and the Kingdom of God

The relationship between the church and the kingdom of God is relevant here. The best description of this relationship involves seeing the church as the manifest representation of the kingdom of God on earth now. In this sense, the church is (1) a sign of the kingdom of God, like a road sign pointing people to heaven, (2) a foretaste of the kingdom of God, giving a taste of heaven on earth through worship, fellowship, and caring, which makes the world want to long for heaven, and (3) an instrument of the kingdom of God, doing God's will on earth as it is in heaven. This view provides a comprehensive picture of the church as the kingdom, making adequate room for the exercise of piety and social justice, moral growth and missional efforts.

I notice all the above in the description of the first church in the book of Acts. I see the following twelve characteristics of the earliest church in Acts 2:42–47:

1. Preaching and teaching
2. Fellowship
3. Breaking of bread
4. Prayers
5. Signs and wonders
6. Sharing time with each other
7. Sharing possessions
8. Eating together

9. Being joyful with simplicity
10. Praise and worship
11. Having favor with all people to share the good news
12. Seeing believers added daily

This church in Jerusalem focused on evangelism and disciple making. No wonder this church went beyond addition to multiplication! Interestingly, this work was not done by people called apostles and deacons. The book of Acts describes people of all walks of life and all kinds of skills (gifts) who turned the world upside down (Acts 17:6). For instance, there were teachers, preachers, and writers like Paul and Apollos, encouragers like Barnabas, attendants like John Mark, faithful companions like Silas, and professionals like physician Luke and tentmakers Aquila and Priscilla.

The ultimate purpose of discipleship is to produce transformed individuals who can minister. Here ministry is not limited to an ordained vocation or full-time Christian service. It is defined as being active and engaged in kingdom priorities as a transformed and transforming follower of Jesus Christ; it is about living as whole persons in a broken world. In other words, it is about living the lifestyle of the kingdom of God.

We cannot do this by our own strength. That is why Jesus told His disciples, "But you will receive power when the Holy Spirit comes on you; and you will be my witnesses in Jerusalem, and in all Judea and Samaria, and to the ends of the earth" (Acts 1:8 NIV). It is the empowerment of the Holy Spirit that makes progressively following Christ possible. Spirit-empowered disciples make disciples. The same Spirit assists the disciple maker and the new disciples. No wonder the weak band of locals in Jerusalem did not make a move until the Holy Spirit came upon them in the Upper Room (Acts 2:4). They obeyed Jesus and refused to leave Jerusalem without the required power.

The Holy Spirit did come. The empowered disciples left Jerusalem and made their way to the ends of the earth, making disciples all over the world. But the task is not complete. The assignment is not over. And thankfully the power has not been withdrawn. We must also receive that same power and be on our way, being disciples, becoming disciple makers, and transforming communities.

CHAPTER 2

TRANSFORMATIONAL DISCIPLESHIP

Then He said to them all, "If anyone desires to come after Me, let him deny himself, and take up his cross daily, and follow Me." (Luke 9:23)

It is an authentic concern that the church and the world look alike in the twenty-first century. This is especially true in America. Known more for the politics of this world than for agape, holiness, and servant leadership, born-again Christians have become ineffective witnesses. Blaming some well-known person or politician and a few misguided preachers does not adequately explain the current situation. Again, evangelical writer Greg Ogden informs us that pastors in general have failed to develop disciples of Jesus; he finds nonclergy decision-makers in the churches also equally responsible for the problem. While the pastor's job description, according to Ephesians 4:10–12, is to equip the saints to do the work of the ministry, the churches have created a system in which pastors are paid to do the ministry and the people are expected to be passive recipients of the pastor's ministry.

The church has also created certain programs that can make it look like disciple making is happening, says Ogden. In the typical American way, we plan to mass produce disciples. We are interested in scaling up production. So we focus on information rather than transformation. We focus on regimentation and synchronization, depending more on high tech than high touch. Without expecting accountability from disciples or disciple makers, we count heads while forgetting that discipleship requires a customized approach to individuals.

Unable or unwilling to invest in individuals, we have divided Christians into two groups: Christians and super Christians. Discipleship is only for the small group of super Christians. Super Christians are expected to pay a cost, but Christians can get cost-free benefits. In this approach, a Christian is a passive believer and a super Christian is active. Christian is a noun. Disciple is a verb!

Pastors are rewarded not for raising followers of Jesus. Instead, church boards look at budgets, buildings, and the number of bodies in seats to measure the effectiveness of pastoral ministry. Churches are busy becoming seeker-friendly to speak to the felt needs of the worldly people. This leads Kent Carson and Mile Leuken to conclude that attracting people to church based on consumer demands is in direct and irredeemable conflict with inviting people "to lose their lives in order to find them!"[12]

We are dealing with a generation of Christians whose faith has become "moralistic therapeutic theism." The central goal of many in this generation is to be happy and feel good about themselves. Be good, feel good, and check in with God when we have a need![13] Rick Warren is right: the church needs to clearly define its purposes and organize around them so there is a sequential process to accomplish them in the lives of believers.[14] Churches and pastors need to reflect on this paradigm-shifting question: How can we grow Christians into self-initiating, fully devoted followers of Jesus Christ by being highly accountable and relational? We need to get back to looking at the Bible as a message book as well as a method book, as Charles Miller has suggested.[15]

Tozer's Challenge

A. W. Tozer believes the church has chosen pietism, literalism, and religious activity as substitutes for discipleship. Literalism lives by the letter of the Word and ignores the spirit. Literalism does not comprehend the lordship of Jesus, the discipleship of the believer, the requirement to live a life of separation from the world, and the need to mortify one's flesh. Literalism attempts to build its temple on the sandy foundation of the religious self. In this perspective, frantic religious activity is now the measure of discipleship. The ultimate test of godliness becomes working for Christ.[16] Christ becomes a project to be promoted or a cause to be served instead of a Lord to be obeyed, says Tozer.

According to Tozer, a transformed disciple carries four marks: (1) a deep reverence for divine things, (2) a great moral sensitivity, (3) a mighty moral discontent, and (4) a consuming spiritual hunger. A true disciple allows the Word to search the heart, has a sense of personal sin, believes Jesus is the only way to overcome guilt, and has a commitment to Jesus Christ as Savior without any reservation. There is no turning back. To true disciples, Christianity is not a part-time commitment. It is life itself.

Tozer points out that the phrase *accept Christ* is not found in the Bible. Accepting Christ should be more than affiliating with a group with common interest. It should represent an attachment to the person of Christ that is revolutionary, complete, and exclusive. Accepting Christ should reverse one's life and transform it completely. One's relationship to Christ should subordinate all other relationships.

Tozer's concept of discipleship requires believers to accept the ways of Jesus as their own, His teachings as their guide, His rejection as their rejection, His cross as their cross, His life as their life, and His future as their future.[17] He believes the idea of accepting Christ only because we need Him as Savior while considering our obedience to Him as negotiable is a heresy. Tozer concludes these attitudes are related to the fact that Christians are influenced by the world rather than by the Word of God. The texture of the modern Christian mind is created by modern entertainment rather than the things of God, he concludes. Only the Word of God can transform a person. Tozer advises, "Read the Word, read often, brood over it, think over it, day and night."[18]

God's purpose for redeeming humanity was that we would allow Him to reproduce the likeness of Jesus Christ in our lives. To Tozer, Christians must live a crucified life. That means, one's natural life has been crucified: "I have been crucified with Christ; it is no longer I who live, but Christ lives in me; and the life which I now live in the flesh I live by faith in the Son of God, who loved me and gave Himself for me" (Gal. 2:20). Disciples carry Christ in them. Christ in believers is the hope of glory (Col. 1:27). There is no difference between clergy and nonclergy when it comes to discipleship. The clergy must also die daily. Coming to the cross means dying to self because the cross is a place of death, says Tozer. He would agree with Bonhoeffer. Christ calls us to come and die.[19] The cross means self-denial, humility, and daily living in obedience to Christ.

A disciple is called to holiness. Holiness is the character of God, and it is also His command. Holiness is moral wholeness. It involves kindness, mercy, purity, blamelessness, and godliness. Faith is not a substitute for action. Christlike conduct is the end result of Christian faith. Discipleship involves both word and deed, both testimony and action.

A Christian is not ready for heaven at the moment of conversion. If it were so, God would have taken us at that moment. Conversion is only the beginning of a journey of faith that involves obedience and transformation until one becomes Christlike. Discipleship is a journey of faith that leads to heaven. Every day is a day of preparation and exercising discipline befitting the destination. Preparation for heaven is a lifetime vocation. The Holy Spirit will guide the disciples in this preparation. Spiritual exercises develop discipline. One grows through discipline, correction, rebuke, and hardship, says Tozer. God designed these for our benefit. God accomplishes spiritual maturity in the followers of Jesus through these.

Discipleship is like membership in an orchestra, Tozer observed. All we do now in our walk with God is a rehearsal. The real concert is coming in the world to come. We will sing there. We can only prepare our garments of righteousness in this life. We will get to wear them at the wedding of the Lamb of God. Meanwhile, we are to link our faith to expression, which means we must go and share our life-giving message with a dying world.

Disciple making is more than preaching and teaching. It requires modeling, which is the best method of teaching available to disciple makers. Modeling happens when we live in a way that people watching us want to resemble us. Modeling works better than other teaching methods based on reward systems and coercion. Modeling affects the values, attitudes, and behaviors of the learner.

Harrington's Elements

Bobby Harrington adds clarity to these matters. He asks us to keep Jesus as the focus of our lives, not discipleship. We must be mindful that discipleship efforts themselves can become a distraction from Christ. Harrington defines a disciple as someone who is following Jesus, being changed by Jesus, and is committed to the mission of Jesus.[20] Disciple making is going, baptizing, and teaching. It is helping people to put their trust in Jesus and follow Jesus (Matt. 28:18–20).

Disciple making is not just the work of pastors. In fact, sermons alone are unlikely to change people at a deeper level and in lasting ways. Disciple making is every believer's job. Just as the people who make the biggest impact on our daily lives are not the most famous ones, it is everyday Christians who can touch us in transforming ways. Harrington points out that Jesus was making disciples of Peter, James, and John long before He was recognized as the Messiah. It appears that disciple making begins before our conversion and continues for the rest of our lives as we follow Jesus.

Transformational discipleship happens not in solo walks but in the community of faith. We do not become disciples outside relationships. There are no self-made disciples or solo discipleship programs. Jesus made disciples through intentional relationships.

Harrington says that there are seven elements to transformational discipleship: (1) relationship, (2) Jesus Christ, (3) intentionality, (4) Bible, (5) Holy Spirit, (6) personal journey, and (7) multiplying. He advises disciple makers to (1) listen to potential disciples, (2) select individuals who are available, faithful, teachable, and reliable, (3) prepare them, (4) engage them, and (5) release them to grow and become disciples and disciple makers.[21] Intentionality is the most important element, according to Harrington, as it separates those who multiply disciples and those who do not.[22]

Harrington points out that Jesus had at least five different types of relationships with people: (1) public (groups larger than one hundred), (2) social (twenty to seventy), (3) personal (eight to fifteen), (4) transparent (two to six), and (5) divinely personal (one on one). Yet disciple making is not a strictly human endeavor. There are three activities involved in this process: (1) the activity of the disciple maker, (2) God's activity through the Word and the Spirit, and (3) the activity of the disciples as they respond to the mentoring of the disciple maker and the work of the Holy Spirit. The work of the disciple maker involves (1) a tool (Bible study, prayer, spiritual disciplines, etc.), (2) a plan in place to avoid boredom and stagnation, and (3) an intentional process or journey.

Dave and Jon Ferguson give a very practical six-step model of this process/journey:[23]

1. I do, you watch, we talk.
2. I do, you help, we talk.
3. You do, I help, we talk.
4. You do, I watch, we talk.
5. You do, someone else watches.
6. I do, someone else watches.

A transformational discipleship journey should not be aimed at the disciple-in-the-making only. It should strategically include the expectations of one disciple making other disciples. Unfortunately, this strategy is missing in most of our churches.

Ogden's Criteria

Greg Ogden concurs and points out that the root of the problem is the wrong message that is being sent out by the church that it is normal to be a Christian without being a disciple of Jesus Christ. Evidence of this is very clear in the Christian community that is engaged in today's full-fledged culture wars. What Bonhoeffer described in his classic book on discipleship has come to pass in our day. What he calls cheap grace has invaded us. Dallas Willard calls today's Christianity barcode Christianity. The church has forgotten that the words *Christian* and *disciple* are interchangeable in the New Testament. This truth should not change in our day.

Just another program will not solve the problem of missing discipleship in the twenty-first-century church. Three vital elements are required to address the challenge. First, we must be willing to stand up for the truth of God's Word in this so-called post-truth period of history. Second, we must be willing to risk relationships for Christ's sake in this age of Facebook friends. Third, we must be willing to submit ourselves to healthy forms of accountability that give authority to Christian peers and discipleship partners to call us to keep our commitments.

Many discipleship programs do not rise above the lowest level of learning, namely, compliance. Some move up to a second level, called identification. At this level the trainee wants to maintain a satisfying relationship with the disciple maker. No significant transformation is involved. The highest level of learning, however, involves internalization. This is when the desired behavior becomes self-directed, second nature, and automatic. Some call this second-order change. In another model, it is the last level of a four-step learning spiral that moves up from (1) unconsciously unskilled to (2) consciously unskilled to (3) consciously skilled to (4) unconsciously skilled.

The disciple maker initiates the invitation to an accountable relationship, guides committed individuals in their journey of faith, prepares tools and assignments to train the disciple, and models a personal life as a disciple in a responsible and transparent way. The most important relationship in the disciple-making process is the one with the Lord Jesus Christ. Spiritual disciplines can give us opportunities to experience the presence of God where we can practice intimacy with the Lord. This process can form us and shape us into the image of Christ. That becomes evident through our vulnerability, truthfulness, and accountability.

According to Greg Ogden, there are five essential criteria to any successful discipleship program: (1) life investment, (2) transferability of values, (3) purposefulness, (4) flexibility, and (5) preparation. He recommends the implementation of a four-part discipleship curriculum: (1) the basics of discipleship in the Bible, (2) the content of the message of the gospel, (3) how to become like Christ with the help of the Holy Spirit, and (4) how to serve Christ and share the good news to make disciples.

Evangelism and Discipleship

Discipleship and evangelism are not the same. Jonathan K. Dodson clarifies the difference. Basically, evangelism is sharing our faith, but disciple making involves both sharing our faith and our lives—failures, successes, disobedience, and obedience. Discipleship is centered on one's relationship to Christ. Activity-centered efforts are no substitute for this dynamic life. The focus should not be on how we perform; it should be on who we are. We should see ourselves as imperfect people who cling to a perfect Christ and are being perfected by the Spirit. We must have an attachment to Christ and to each other. Our relationships should have grace at the center of them rather than rules, says Dodson.

Discipleship must be centered in the gospel. If evangelism is the initial making of disciples, discipleship is the continual making of disciples. Discipleship is an integrated three-dimensional concept. "We are to go in the power of the gospel, baptize into the grace of the gospel, and teach the person of the gospel," says Dodson.[24] The gospel integrates evangelism and discipleship by announcing a grace that saves and sanctifies the disciples. A similar integration is needed between personal piety and social justice activism. Currently, some disciples are only concerned about personal holiness while others only care about missional concerns and social justice issues. Unfortunately, according to Dodson, pious disciples (whom he calls vertical disciples) withdraw from the world, while missional disciples (labeled horizontal disciples) just want to engage the world. The first group focuses on who God is; the second group focuses on what He does in the world. The solution to this dichotomy, according to Dodson, is not trying to balance these two in our personal lives, but to focus on Jesus.[25] Jesus is Lord means He is Savior and King. We must trust Him as Savior and serve Him as King. We serve Him by serving others.

Our mission is about making disciples. This mission is God's mission. We must embrace it. Mission, however, is not just programs and activities but life itself. As God the Father sent the Son via the incarnation and God the Spirit was sent into the world, God the Holy Spirit has empowered the church and sent the church into all the world (in Oral Roberts's words, "into every person's world").

Legalism is a real problem among Christians. It is the tendency to measure our worth by how well we perform. It is measured by and driven by performance. We may notice that Jesus did not spend much time looking for affirmation from His performance. Can you imagine if He waited around to get compliments for turning water into wine! Maybe He did not need to depend on performance for self-esteem. His Father had affirmed Him way before His first public "performance" by saying, "This is My beloved Son, in whom I am well pleased" (Matt. 3:17).

The human tendency is to turn everything into a competition. We also like to earn our way and pay for our salvation by performance. The fact is that salvation is available only by grace. No performance is required. Dodson says that confession is not a bargaining chip we can cash in to obtain a clear conscience. Our forgiveness has already been bought by Jesus. We freely receive it by grace and "procure his purchased forgiveness through confession." We do not need to perform spiritually to impress God morally or missionally. Anything we use to replace Jesus is an idol. Even holiness and moral behavior can become an idol.

We still must obey God, because God's forgiveness frees us from judgment, not from obedience. As Jesus has already impressed God, we do not have to try to impress Him. What we need is not rule keeping (religion) or rule breaking (rebellion). Instead, embrace the gospel that binds us to Jesus Christ. This is not cheap grace. Truly this is costly grace.

What motivates a true disciple is true affection for God. It is delight in God that not only believes in God but also tastes Him.

Repentance is not a once-in-a-lifetime experience. Repentance is not just an admission ticket to heaven. For a disciple, it is a way of life. It is a lifestyle. In fact, according to the late New York pastor Tim Keller, repentance is the best sign we are growing into the character of Jesus.

One cannot practice true holiness without the help of the Holy Spirit. I recall Dr. Henry Lederle, a colleague at Oral

Roberts University, saying that many Christians are functional binitarians. While identifying themselves as trinitarians, they ignore or neglect the work of the Holy Spirit in their lives, Lederle said. The power and presence of the Holy Spirit are the key to living a holy life. I will conclude this chapter with a statement from Oral Roberts: "Wholeness is holiness and holiness is wholeness."

CHAPTER 3

SPIRITUAL GROWTH: A DEVELOPMENTAL JOURNEY

But grow in the grace and knowledge of our Lord and Savior Jesus Christ. To Him be the glory both now and forever. Amen. (2 Pet. 3:18)

The church in the twenty-first century is in crisis across the world. It has to do with the failure in its main business, which is to make disciples (not adherents) and help them to grow spiritually. Underneath several major issues within the church in general and within the evangelical and pentecostal communities in particular is this matter of missing biblical discipleship and biblically sound efforts to help believers grow. Even churches that claim an increase in their membership cannot boast an increase in the spiritual maturity of their members. Church growth and the spiritual growth of churchgoers are not the same.

Pastors I have spoken to agree with this diagnosis, but there is no evidence this concern is translating into any significant, widely implemented remedial actions. We have many programs to help people with all sorts of problems but not enough to guide them in their growth and development as disciples of Jesus Christ. We are failing to move people from church membership to discipleship to spiritual formation. Unfortunately, we live in a "Christian" country where only 20 percent of church members show up to worship weekly. This is not a glowing testimony.

I recall looking anxiously at an ultrasound image of our first grandson several months before he was born. So I can imagine God looking intensely into our souls to see if the image of His Son is being formed in us. The purpose of discipleship is spiritual formation, and spiritual formation is measured in terms of Christlikeness in believers: "For whom He foreknew, He also predestined to be conformed to the image of his Son, that He might be the firstborn among many brethren" (Rom. 8:29). I heard the bishop of the Eastern Orthodox Church say at what was considered the largest Christian convention in Asia at Maramon, India, in 2023 that true discipleship is growing from the image of God into the likeness of Christ.

However, spiritual maturity among Christians is nothing to brag about currently. I recall one of the leaders at Oral Roberts University say that many Christians are as Christian as a person in a monkey suit at the circus is a monkey. This must change. God expects His children to grow in grace and in the knowledge of the Lord Jesus Christ (2 Pet. 3:18). Just having a form of godliness without its power is not real Christianity.

The Bible calls for growth and wholeness. It advises us to be complete in Jesus. We are called to grow into the fullness of Christ and to become mature enough to make disciples and to minister to those in need.

Fowler, Aden, and Westerhoff

Studies in the stages of faith by James Fowler at Emory University and others have examined this matter closely. These studies seem to follow the different dimensions of spiritual growth—the content of faith or the cognitive (thinking) aspect of faith, the affective dimension that deals with the emotional and commitment aspects of faith, and the practical and behavioral aspects of faith. Fowler probably gives the best model of the stages of faith, especially from the thinking aspect of faith development. He believes there are seven stages:[26]

1. Undifferentiated faith: the disposition to trust in infancy.
2. Intuitive/projective faith: prelogical faith in childhood based on stories and images.
3. Mythical/literal faith: beginning to think logically about one's faith to order one's world in childhood and beyond.
4. Synthetic/conventional faith: largely unreflective synthesis of one's beliefs in support of one's identity in adolescence.
5. Individualizing/reflective faith: critical reflection of one's beliefs and practices in youth and adulthood.
6. Paradoxical/consolidation faith: awareness of multiple interpretations of faith and acknowledgment of having paradoxes in one's faith in midlife.

7. Universalizing faith: where one is free of certain limitations to spend one's self in love, according to Fowler, working to overcome division, oppression, and brutality in the world. This is not limited to a particular religion and includes, for example, Mahatma Gandhi as well as Martin Luther King Jr. This is a challenging proposition from an explicitly evangelical perspective.

Fowler's psychosocial model, like Erik Erikson's human development model, is related to human life stages. Erikson concluded that human development involves eight stages. The first four stages are in infancy and childhood, stage five is in adolescence, and the remaining are in adulthood. Erikson believed each stage of life is characterized by a psychosocial conflict to be handled in a healthy way and resolved. There are negative implications when one unsuccessfully leaves a stage. However, these issues can be resolved later in life if one wishes to address them. Erikson's psychosocial model lists the following eight stages (and associated issues):[27]

1. Trust versus mistrust (learning to trust, to have faith in another person)
2. Autonomy versus shame (developing autonomy or self-regulation)
3. Initiative versus guilt (learning to initiate)
4. Industry versus inferiority (developing confidence)
5. Identity versus role confusion (discovering and affirming one's self)
6. Intimacy versus isolation (establishing proper relational distance from others)

7. Generativity versus stagnation (investing in the next generation or drying up in a self-centered life)
8. Integrity versus despair (living with hope in spite of challenges in later life)

Unlike Fowler, Leroy Aden related Erikson's eight stages more directly to Christian faith in the following way:[28]

1. Faith as trust in infancy
2. Faith as courage in early childhood
3. Faith as obedience in preschool
4. Faith as assent in school age
5. Faith as identity in adolescence
6. Faith as self-surrender in young adulthood
7. Faith as unconditional caring in midlife
8. Faith as unconditional acceptance

In his book *Will Our Children Have Faith?* John Westerhoff presented a four-stage model of faith development:[29]

1. Experienced faith (infancy to early adolescence)
2. Affirmative faith (late adolescence)
3. Searching faith (young adulthood)
4. Owned faith (midlife to old age)

The Christian life is a matter of faith and the research mentioned above demonstrates that discipleship is a journey of faith. One needs a good biblical understanding of the term *faith* to grasp the thinking (knowledge, content) aspect of spiritual growth. Let us begin with a brief survey of the biblical use of the word *faith*.

Faith in the Bible

After telling the story of the judge who did not fear God or regard man but answered a widow's request to establish that God answers the prayer of faith, no matter how hard the request or how delayed the answer might be (Luke 18:1–8), Jesus asked, "Nevertheless, when the Son of Man comes, will He really find faith on the earth?" (v. 8). Jesus expected a shortage of faith in the world in the last days. Paul told his disciple and young pastor Timothy to be an example in faith: "Let no one despise your youth, but be an example to the believers in word, in conduct, in love, in spirit, in faith, in purity" (1 Tim. 4:12). Obviously, God honors faith, and Timothy was expected to keep the faith, which comes by hearing of the Word of God: "So then faith comes by hearing, and hearing by the word of God" (Rom. 10:17).

The Bible actually defines faith: "Now faith is the substance of things hoped for, the evidence of things not seen" (Heb. 11:1). God loves to honor faith. He responds to faith. Jesus said, "Most assuredly, I say to you, he who believes in Me, the works that I do he will do also; and greater works than these he will do, because I go to My Father" (John 14:12). Jesus was moved by faith. His conversation with the disciples who failed to heal the sick boy in Matthew 17:19–21 reveals this:

> Then the disciples came to Jesus privately and said, "Why could we not cast it out?"
>
> So Jesus said to them, "Because of your unbelief; for assuredly, I say to you, if you have faith as a mustard seed, you will say to this mountain, 'Move from here to

> there,' and it will move; and nothing will be impossible for you. However, this kind does not go out except by prayer and fasting."

Faith appears to be the currency of the kingdom of God. Listen to the words Jesus spoke to the centurion who had a sick servant: "'Go your way; and as you have believed, so let it be done for you.' And his servant was healed that same hour" (Matt. 8:13).

The Bible gives several illustrations of faith. In Abraham's case, faith was taking a step based on God's Word without knowing his destination: "By faith Abraham obeyed when he was called to go out to the place which he would receive as an inheritance. And he went out, not knowing where he was going" (Heb. 11:8). Noah built an ark on dry land before he really knew what rain was: "By faith Noah, being divinely warned of things not yet seen, moved with godly fear, prepared an ark for the saving of his household, by which he condemned the world and became heir of the righteousness which is according to faith" (Heb. 11:7). The woman in the New Testament who had a chronic condition exercised her faith a different way. She "came from behind and touched the border of His garment. And immediately her flow of blood stopped" (Luke 8:44). A blind man expressed his faith by following Jesus' instruction. John reports that Jesus "spat on the ground and made clay with the saliva; and He anointed the eyes of the blind man with the clay. And He said to him, 'Go, wash in the pool of Siloam' (which is translated, Sent). So he went and washed, and came back seeing" (John 9:6–7). Similarly, the ten lepers who needed healing took off to see the priests based on faith in the command of Jesus: "And so it was that as they went, they were cleansed" (Luke 17:14).

Faith has many benefits, according to the Bible. First, faith pleases God: "But without faith it is impossible to please Him, for he who comes to God must believe that He is, and that He is a rewarder of those who diligently seek Him" (Heb. 11:6). Faith justifies sinners: "Therefore we conclude that a man is justified by faith apart from the deeds of the law" (Rom. 3:28). Faith sanctifies believers. Listen to the story of the first council of the church in Jerusalem that determined the destiny of the Gentiles:

> Now the apostles and elders came together to consider this matter. And when there had been much dispute, Peter rose up and said to them: "Men and brethren, you know that a good while ago God chose among us, that by my mouth the Gentiles should hear the word of the gospel and believe. So God, who knows the heart, acknowledged them by giving them the Holy Spirit, just as He did to us, and made no distinction between us and them, purifying their hearts by faith." (Acts 15:6–9)

Faith offers comfort and calm to the believer. Jesus told His disciples: "Let not your heart be troubled; you believe in God, believe also in Me" (John 14:1). Faith gives victory over the world. The apostle John said: "For whatever is born of God overcomes the world. And this is the victory that has overcome the world—our faith. Who is he who overcomes the world, but he who believes that Jesus is the Son of God?" (1 John 5:4–5). And faith will lead believers to heaven. Abraham's testimony is a clear example of this anticipation: "By faith Abraham obeyed when he was called to go out to the place which he would receive as an inheritance. And he went out, not knowing where he was going. By faith he dwelt in the land of promise as in a foreign country, dwelling in tents with Isaac and Jacob, the heirs with him of the same promise; for he waited for the city which has foundations, whose builder and maker is God" (Heb. 11:8–10). One can learn about faith from Abraham, who was called the father of all believers. By faith he made a move without knowing the destination, obeyed God's command without knowing the reason, waited in tents without knowing how long the waiting would be, and received the promises of God without knowing how.

Paul told Timothy the essentials of what he was to believe: "This is a faithful saying and worthy of all acceptance, that Christ Jesus came into the world to save sinners, of whom I am chief" (1 Tim. 1:15). Paul elaborated this subject to Titus, who also was expected to affirm this faith:

> But when the kindness and the love of God our Savior toward man appeared, not by works of righteousness which we have done, but according to His mercy He saved us, through the washing of regeneration and renewing of the Holy Spirit, whom He poured out on us abundantly through Jesus Christ our Savior, that having been justified by His grace we should become heirs according to the hope of eternal life.

> This is a faithful saying, and these things I want you to affirm constantly, that those who have believed in God should be careful to maintain good works. These things are good and profitable to men. (Titus 3:4–8)

Doctrines (the content of what one believes) are most important. For example, Paul advised Timothy again and again:

> Till I come, give attention to reading, to exhortation, to doctrine. (1 Tim. 4:13)
>
> Take heed to yourself and to the doctrine. Continue in them, for in doing this you will save both yourself and those who hear you. (1 Tim. 4:16)
>
> Fight the good fight of faith, lay hold on eternal life, to which you were also called and have confessed the good confession in the presence of many witnesses. (1 Tim. 6:12)

While keeping doctrinal purity, the disciples must pay attention to the lifestyle dimension of their faith. Jude said, "But you, beloved, building yourselves up on your most holy faith, praying in the Holy Spirit, keep yourselves in the love of God, looking for the mercy of our Lord Jesus Christ unto eternal life" (Jude 1:20–21).

Followers of Jesus are to fight for their faith. Plenty of reasons are given for this requirement. First, in the last days some will depart from the faith: "Now the Spirit expressly says that in latter times some will depart from the faith, giving heed to deceiving spirits and doctrines of demons, speaking lies in hypocrisy, having their own conscience seared with a hot iron, forbidding to marry, and commanding to abstain from foods which God created to be received with thanksgiving by those who believe and know the truth" (1 Tim. 4:1–3). Additionally, some will deny their faith through their lifestyle: "But if anyone does not provide for his own, and especially for those of his household, he has denied the faith and is worse than an unbeliever" (1 Tim. 5:8).

One must fight for the faith because it is possible to lose it (1 Tim. 5:11–12), that is, one can follow a different faith or "another gospel." Love of money can cause some to give up their faith: "For the love of money is a root of all kinds of evil, for which some have strayed from the faith in their greediness, and pierced themselves through with many sorrows" (1 Tim. 6:10). Others can be seduced away: "Guard what was committed to your trust, avoiding the profane and idle babblings and contradictions of what is falsely called knowledge—by professing it some have strayed concerning the faith" (1 Tim. 6:20–21). The story of Demas who forsook Paul and the mission is well known; Paul reported, he "loved this present world, and has departed for Thessalonica" (2 Tim. 4:10). Such individuals not only lose their faith, but they also can overthrow the faith of others: "And their message will spread like cancer. Hymenaeus and Philetus are of this sort, who have strayed concerning the truth, saying that the resurrection is already past; and they overthrow the faith of some" (2 Tim. 2:17–18).

Paul's testimony about his faith should be what every disciple should hope for: "I have fought the good fight, I have finished the race, I have kept the faith. Finally, there is laid up for me the crown of righteousness, which the Lord, the righteous Judge, will give to me on that Day, and not to me only but also to all who have loved His appearing" (2 Tim. 4:7–8).

Faith is a way of knowing like knowing through seeing, hearing, touching, tasting, and smelling: "Now faith is the substance of things hoped for, the evidence of things not seen" (Heb. 11:1). We receive knowledge through the Word and the Spirit, which is made clear in Paul's letters. "So then faith comes by hearing, and hearing by the word of God," he wrote the Romans about receiving knowledge through the Word (Rom. 10:17). To the Galatians he wrote, "That the blessing of Abraham might come upon the Gentiles in Christ Jesus, that we might receive the promise of the Spirit through faith" (Gal. 3:14). He made this claim to the Corinthians also:

> But we speak the wisdom of God in a mystery, the hidden wisdom which God ordained before the ages for our glory, which none of the rulers of this age knew; for had they known, they would not have crucified the Lord of glory.
>
> But as it is written:
>
> "Eye has not seen, nor ear heard,
> Nor have entered into the heart of man
> The things which God has prepared for those who love Him."
>
> But God has revealed them to us through His Spirit. For the Spirit searches all things, yes, the deep things of God. (1 Cor. 2:7–10)

Knowing through the Spirit is called discernment: "But the natural man does not receive the things of the Spirit of God, for they are foolishness to him; nor can he know them, because they are spiritually discerned" (1 Cor. 2:14). Discernment is listed as a gift of the Spirit in 1 Corinthians 12:7–11.

Knowing is also possible through the church, the community of faith. For instance, concerning the gift of interpretation, Paul said, "He who speaks in a tongue edifies himself, but he who prophesies edifies the church. I wish you all spoke with tongues, but even more that you prophesied; for he who prophesies is greater than he who speaks with tongues, unless indeed he interprets, that the church may receive edification. But now, brethren, if I come to you speaking with tongues, what shall I profit you unless I speak to you either by revelation, by knowledge, by prophesying, or by teaching?" (1 Cor. 14:4–6).

Faith is not only a way of knowing, but it is also a means of empowerment. Paul said to the Corinthians: "For the message of the cross is foolishness to those who are perishing, but to us who are being saved it is the power of God" (1 Cor. 1:18). He said to the Romans: "For I am not ashamed of the gospel of Christ, for it is the power of God to salvation for everyone who believes, for the Jew first and also for the Greek" (Rom. 1:16). Peter confirmed this way of empowerment: "Blessed be the God and Father of our Lord Jesus Christ, who according to His abundant mercy has begotten us again to a living hope through the resurrection of Jesus Christ from the dead, to an inheritance incorruptible and undefiled and that does not fade away, reserved in heaven for you, who are kept by the power of God through faith for salvation ready to be revealed in the last time" (1 Pet. 1:3–5).

Faith is also a motivation for action. James gives the best instruction regarding this:

> What does it profit, my brethren, if someone says he has faith but does not have works? Can faith save him? . . .
>
> But someone will say, "You have faith, and I have works." Show me your faith without your works, and I will show you my faith by my works. . . . Was not Abraham our father justified by works when he offered Isaac his son on the altar? Do you see that faith was working together with his works, and by works faith was made perfect? . . . You see then that a man is justified by works, and not by faith only. (James 2:14, 18, 21–22, 24)

Here is a way to summarize discipleship in terms of faith development. We are saved by faith (Eph. 2:8). We live by faith: "For in it the righteousness of God is revealed from faith to faith; as it is written, 'The just shall live by faith'" (Rom. 1:17). We walk by faith: "For we walk by faith, not by sight" (2 Cor. 5:7). We overcome the world, flesh, and the devil by faith: "For whatever is born of God overcomes the world. And this is the victory that has overcome the world—our faith. Who is he who overcomes the world, but he who believes that Jesus is the Son of God" (1 John 5:4–5). And we will die in faith as we read about the saints listed in Hebrews: "These all died in faith, not having received the promises, but having seen them afar off were assured of them, embraced them and confessed that they were strangers and pilgrims on the earth" (11:13).

I believe we can discern certain predictable stages of spiritual growth and maturity in Paul's writings. He sees disciples progressing through these stages: natural, carnal, and spiritual. The Corinthians were natural: "But the natural man does not receive the things of the Spirit of God, for they are foolishness to him; nor can he know them, because they are spiritually discerned" (1 Cor. 2:14). He defined carnal in Romans and called the Corinthians by that name:

> For to be carnally minded is death, but to be spiritually minded is life and peace. Because the carnal mind is enmity against God; for it is not subject to the law of God, nor indeed can be. (Rom. 8:6–7)
>
> And I, brethren, could not speak to you as to spiritual people but as to carnal, as to babes in Christ. I fed you with milk and not with solid food; for until now you were not able to receive it, and even now you are still not able; for you are still carnal. For where there are envy, strife, and divisions among you, are you not carnal and behaving like mere men? (1 Cor. 3:1–3)

Emotions, Commitment, and Behavior

Discipleship is not just about the knowledge of one's faith or one's cognitive development in spirituality. A disciple is a learner and a follower at the same time. Emotional maturity is vital to spiritual growth. Peter Scazzero's writings explored the emotional dimension of healthy spirituality, leadership, and discipleship. He provided biblically sound and practical ways to live as emotionally healthy Christians and leaders who can develop emotionally healthy disciples and grow emotionally healthy churches. He stated that real spiritual maturity is not possible until one intentionally chooses to live an emotionally healthy life. This is not an easy choice or decision. In his book *The Emotionally Healthy Church*, Scazzero claims: "Emotional health and spiritual maturity are inseparable. It is not possible to be spiritually mature while remaining emotionally immature."[30]

Many Christians live superficial lives. Scazzero challenged Christians to choose a deeper way to live. He presented the following seven principles to help pastors and believers to live emotionally healthy lives:

1. Look beneath the surface.
2. Break the power of the past.
3. Live in brokenness and vulnerability.
4. Receive the gift of limits.
5. Embrace grieving and loss.
6. Make incarnation your model for loving well.
7. Slow down to live with integrity.[31]

Professor Charles Farah of Oral Roberts University dealt with the commitment and behavioral dimensions of faith from a pentecostal-charismatic perspective. He called his model "types" of faith. According to Farah, the lowest level of discipleship is called *historical faith*. This is faith based on other individuals or one's church affiliation. In this stage, one sees oneself as a part of a denomination or a heritage. Faith is not personally owned; it is corporate in nature, with minimum personal commitment. Farah called the second level *temporary faith*. This is a stage in which one's faith is activated but remains so only for a short period. Like the seeds that fell among thorns in Jesus' parable, the spiritual awakening is temporary. The third type is called *saving faith*. Here one experiences new birth in Christ. Unfortunately, many are stuck at this stage for a long time. They claim to be Christians, but there is no spiritual growth taking place. Many people at the congregational level of Christian life are at this stage.

Farah calls the fourth level *faith for miracles*. One is open to the work of the Spirit in this stage, but faith here is something one must "work up." It is not something that flows easily through one's life. This is where one's faith is built on rules, regulations, and formulas. The fifth level is called *gift faith*. Here one is growing in God and is allowing the gifts of the Spirit to manifest in and through one's life. Faith is not something worked up in this level; it is truly a gift received from God.

There are people who reach the level of gift faith, but they do not have the character to match the gifts. They often self-sabotage due to a lack of discipline. Farah called the sixth level of faith *fruit faith*. This denotes active discipleship and testifies to significant spiritual growth. True discipleship changes one's character and behavior. Gifts of the Spirit are given, but the fruits of the Spirit are cultivated. This cultivation involves effort, and it happens only through a process that involves others. No one reaches this stage in isolation and through solo practice. This is where the church can improve by providing more intentional opportunities for potential disciples to grow.

The seventh and highest level of growth in discipleship involves the type of faith Farah called *ministry faith*. At this stage, one is able to minister to others instead of being preoccupied with one's own needs. A mature disciple is able to share the gospel with others and nurture them. In some other models of discipleship, this stage is called workers, leaders, etc. I prefer Farah's model, because it focuses on ministry, without confining it to working or leading. One realizes at this stage that faith is not just for receiving something from God, rather it is for giving something to others. The highest level of faith is about giving, not receiving; it is about ministering to others, not expecting ministry from others.

As we have seen, spiritual growth involves a cognitive aspect of faith, a commitment aspect of faith, and a behavioral aspect of faith. Growth in these three areas impacts all three dimensions of our personality—cognitive, affective, and behavioral, or knowledge, attitude, and practice. We must disciple and mentor Christians, especially new believers, to reach their full potential in all of these areas as followers of Jesus. This is consistent with Paul's understanding of ministry in Ephesians 4:11–13: "And He Himself gave some to be apostles, some prophets, some evangelists, and some pastors and teachers, for the equipping of the saints for the work of ministry, for the edifying of the body of Christ, till we all come to the unity of the faith and of the knowledge of the Son of God, to a perfect man, to the measure of the stature of the fullness of Christ."

Pruyser and Healthy Faith

I found a helpful way for Christians to monitor themselves to see how they are growing and developing as disciples based on what Paul Pruyser, in his book *Minister as a Diagnostician*,[32] calls pastoral diagnostic themes. These themes that are normally used to make spiritual diagnoses by pastoral counselors allow us to monitor ourselves in terms of our spiritual health as disciples.

Pruyser's themes provide the practical factors listed below to monitor our health and well-being as disciples of Jesus Christ.

1. **Awareness of the holy.** Healthy Christians must be aware of the presence of a holy God in their life. People often describe their life issues in ways that one wonders where God is in respect to their situation. Our awareness of the presence of God in our life is a sign of healthy discipleship.
2. **Sense of providence.** Providence is a theological term that means God the Creator takes care of His creation. Healthy disciples have an assurance that God will meet their needs, so they can face the challenges and issues of life from a position of confidence. God's providence covers His entire creation. A sense of providence enables us to live by faith, in the knowledge that God will supply all our needs through Christ Jesus (Phil. 4:19).
3. **Stance of faith.** Growing disciples look at their world through the eyes of faith. Just as eyeglasses affect one's vision, faith affects one's view of life. Healthy disciples walk by faith and not by sight alone. Faith enables us to believe in God's providence; faith believes that God is faithful. When we consider all the "by faith" statements in Hebrews 11, it becomes clear the author is describing life as an adventure of faith. Healthy disciples have this type of faith.
4. **Experience of gratefulness.** Healthy disciples live a thankful life in which their attitude is based on gratitude.

Unfortunately, gratefulness is a rare commodity in an affluent society. Healthy disciples enjoy God's grace with gratitude. Gratitude does not depend on the size of the gift; it flows out of our relationship with the giver.

5. **Process of repenting.** All born-again Christians believe God has forgiven their sins. The Christian life is a forgiven life. All of us, however, are subject to committing sins of commission and omission. This means we must live with an attitude of repentance. The ability to experience *metanoia* (repentance), to ask for forgiveness, and to live in humility are evidence of a spiritually wholesome life.
6. **Feeling of communion.** The Bible speaks about the communion of the saints; a sense of community fosters communion. Growing disciples experience communion with God and with the members of the community of faith. This extends beyond the sacrament of communion to a sense of belonging and intimacy within the local community of faith and the extended family of God. Healthy disciples have the capacity for intimacy with God and others. All of us have met long-term members of a particular church who describe the church as "their" (other people's) church. Regardless of the cause, this attitude reflects the absence of a sense of communion with the body of Christ. Having a sense of belonging and community is a sign of spiritual growth and development.
7. **Sense of vocation.** In the Christian life, all are called by God; therefore, all Christians must see their life's work, whatever that might be, as a calling. In this

> perspective, both "professional" ministry and "secular" employment become vocations. We are called to do all as unto Christ (Eph. 6:5). Healthy disciples see their life's calling as a vocation.

Pruyser's themes are important indicators of true discipleship. We will benefit from examining our lives with respect to these themes as they are measures of our spiritual growth and development as disciples of Jesus Christ. After all, as disciples, we must "grow in the grace and knowledge of our Lord and Savior Jesus Christ" (2 Pet. 3:18).

The Holy Spirit and Discipleship

Discipleship is a journey that leads to spiritual growth and life transformation. This does not happen without the work of the Holy Spirit. True disciples allow the Holy Spirit to work in and through them. The book of Acts testifies the Spirit did four specific things in the lives of the earliest disciples.

1. The Spirit empowered the disciples.
2. The Spirit expanded their vision.
3. The Spirit enabled them to embrace strangers.
4. The Spirit transformed the disciples.

We also must allow this to happen in our lives. So let's look at each of the Spirit's workings in the book of Acts.

The Spirit empowers. The Holy Spirit is the source of power to witness beyond our abilities. The disciples who waited in the Upper Room and received the Holy Spirit on the day of pentecost were empowered by the Spirit. The Holy Spirit became the power for these early Christians to witness beyond their abilities. A new boldness possessed this petrified group

(4:20; 5:29; 7:54–60; 9:31) as a result of receiving the Holy Spirit. Signs and wonders took place beyond the ministries of the leaders and through the work of others in near and far places (8:8). The Spirit began to move in places like Antioch, through ordinary persons who were not apostles, the presumed administrators of the divine work.

The Spirit expands vision. When the Spirit came, Christian faith moved from being local to global; the disciples experienced an expansion of their vision. It seems the things Jesus had taught them began to make more sense to them after they were filled with the Spirit. They watched the 120 people in the Upper Room become three thousand believers in a single day. The community grew and its vision and mission expanded. The whole world was in Jerusalem on the day of pentecost, and Jerusalem was about to go to the whole world. The church was adding members at the beginning, but soon it seemed to be multiplying membership.

The Holy Spirit impacted the worldview of the early disciples. They used to be local people with limited vision. Pentecost extended the disciples' vision and launched them toward people and faraway places they had not considered before.

The Spirit enables us to embrace strangers. The Spirit brought cultural strangers into the church, and the church was able to embrace them. This was not always the case with the disciples. The Spirit began to remove internal and external hindrances within individuals and in the community to grow the church. Distance was no longer a barrier. Samaria and Antioch were reached. Gender was not a barrier. Women were included in the life and ministry of the community. Sons and daughters were prophesying (18:26; 21:9). Titles were not a barrier to relationships and ministry. Deacons, not just apostles, were ministering signs and wonders. Race was not a barrier. The 120 in the Upper Room in Acts 2 were basically a Jewish group. In Acts 3 a handicapped person came in. In Acts 6 Greek women were being taken care of. Samaritans were included in Acts 8. The Ethiopian, an African, also came in Acts 8. The Gentile Cornelius was welcomed in Acts 10. Lydia, the European businesswoman, was included in Acts 16. The Spirit enabled the local group to embrace the world and demonstrate global diversity!

The Spirit transforms. The Holy Spirit transformed individuals and communities in the first-century church. Communities were transformed in Jerusalem and Ephesus as individuals touched by the Spirit were transformed. Peter's life is an excellent case study of this. Peter was the disciple who said no to several key initiatives. He had said no to the crucifixion (Matt. 16:22–23). He was on record as against Jesus' washing his feet (John 13:8). He definitely said no to the idea of going to the house of a Gentile like Cornelius (Acts 10:14). He was, however, persuaded by unbelievable divine appointments to visit Cornelius. He preached Jesus at the house of this Gentile, and the results completely surprised him and everyone else involved.

> While Peter was still speaking these words, the Holy Spirit came on all who heard the message. The circumcised believers who had come with Peter were astonished

> that the gift of the Holy Spirit had been poured out even on Gentiles. For they heard them speaking in tongues and praising God.
>
> Then Peter said, "Surely no one can stand in the way of their being baptized with water. They have received the Holy Spirit just as we have." (10:44–47 NIV)

Peter was transformed by the work of the Holy Spirit in him. After the visit to Cornelius's house, he was never the same again. His transformation was significant and strategic for the purposes of God. Later, this apostle who was adamant about having Jewish prerequisites for Christian initiation defended the opposite position on diversity at the Jerusalem conference (15:6–10). Amazing, indeed! He was transformed by the Spirit. Disciples are transformed by the power of the Holy Spirit.

Disciples of Jesus Christ are under the authority of the Lord and minister to others in the authority given to them by Him. True disciples are sanctified by God's Word and the blood of Jesus Christ and are transformed by the power of His Spirit.

Four Portraits

I looked for additional clues for spiritual growth and maturity in the book of Acts. I read the book with this question in mind: What does a mature Christian look like in Acts? I found four not-so-hidden portraits emerging.

1. Mature disciples listen to the Spirit, obey the Spirit, and reach out to others even in difficult situations.

Philip is an example for this. He was a very ordinary church member who was elected to be a deacon to serve at the tables.

We are told he was a man of honest report and full of the Holy Spirit and wisdom. While serving others and caring for people, he heard the Spirit say that he had to go to the Gaza desert road. He followed the Spirit and met an Ethiopian eunuch on his way back to his homeland. He ran behind the chariot and was invited in to explain a biblical passage. The instruction led to the eunuch's conversion and baptism in the desert. He went home rejoicing, becoming the first missionary to Africa before Europe received the good news! The Spirit took Philip to his next assignment in Azotus, a city on the Mediterranean Sea (Acts 8:26–40).

Philip had all the reasons in the world not to go to the desert road to meet a foreigner, a man of a different race. He went outside of his comfort zone. Starting by walking, he ran and eventually flew! Spiritual growth involves caring, sharing, leaving one's comfort zone, and reaching out to strangers with the good news of Jesus. They listen to the Spirit, obey the Spirit, and willingly go into the desert.

2. Mature disciples overcome their fears and minister to others.

Ananias is a good example. Saul had a bad reputation as a persecutor of Christians. Ananias was called a disciple (Acts 9:10). He had heard frightening stories about Saul and never expected to meet him. Then God spoke to him. "Arise, and go into the street which is called Straight, and enquire in the house of Judas for one called Saul, of Tarsus: for, behold, he prayeth" (v. 11 KJV). Ananias expressed understandable hesitation: "Lord, I have heard by many of this man, how much evil he hath done to thy saints at Jerusalem: and here he hath authority from the chief priests to bind all that call on thy name" (vv. 9:13–14 KJV). But the Lord told him, "Go thy way: for he is a chosen vessel unto me, to bear my name before the Gentiles, and kings, and the children of Israel" (v. 15 KJV). Ananias overcame his fear and went to Straight Street and met Saul, who had been blinded as a result of his encounter on the road. He laid hands on the young man and spoke in the most loving way to him: "'Brother Saul, the Lord Jesus, who appeared to you on the road as you came, has sent me that you may receive your sight and be filled with the Holy Spirit.' Immediately there fell from his eyes something like scales, and he received his sight at once; and he arose and was baptized" (vv. 17–18).

Ananias was a mature disciple who demonstrated spiritual growth by overcoming his fears and apprehensions to minister to a person in need. Our hurting world desperately needs followers of Jesus who are like Ananias, a man about whom we still know very little.

3. Mature disciples overcome their traditions and ethnic pride and embrace people of all backgrounds.

The apostle Peter, despite his well-documented impulsive personality, is the best example of this in Acts. He had said no to the cross when Jesus announced His impending crucifixion (Matt. 16:22). He was also against the idea of Jesus' washing his disciples' feet as a gesture of servant leadership (John 13:8). He had also said a strong no to the invitation to go to the house of the Gentile Cornelius (Acts 10:14). However, he reluctantly went to Cornelius's house and began to speak about Jesus.

While he was speaking, to the surprise of everyone present, the Spirit fell on everyone who was listening to his message. The Holy Spirit who moved unpredictably like wind, water, and fire surprised Peter and all who had accompanied him to Caesarea, and this experience impacted him and transformed him in a way beyond everything that had happened on the day of pentecost. Peter ordered all the uncircumcised Gentiles to be baptized that day.

The evidence of Peter's profound change manifested later when he gave a convincing argument at the Jerusalem Council to accept Gentiles into the church without imposing circumcision on them, as many Jewish believers and powerful leaders insisted (Acts 15:6–18). He was able to overcome his prejudice and embrace a stranger whom God had brought into his life and thereby open the door to the Gentile world to enter the family of God. The impact of that transformation and the consequences of the council's decision are still felt across the world. I don't know that if that decision was not made, the size of the Christian church would be what it is today. Spiritual growth is not optional. The future of the church and the world depends on whether the disciples of Jesus will grow in their faith.

Race should not be a barrier to fellowship. The story of the church in Acts includes people of all backgrounds. Samaritans and Greeks (8:4–8, 14–17; 11:19–20), an Ethiopian (8:36), and Gentiles are all part of the family of God, enjoying the full benefit of belonging to the family of God. Looking through the book of Acts chapter by chapter, I notice the following:

Acts 2: Mostly Jews
Acts 3: Handicapped

Acts 6: Greeks

Acts 8: Samaritans

Acts 8: Ethiopian

Acts 10: Gentile Cornelius

Acts 16: Lydia the European businesswoman

The earliest disciples of Jesus overcame their prejudices and their prejudice-based traditions and reached out to the people whom God brought to them.

4. Mature disciples pray in chains (trust God in difficult situations) and sing even in prison (can maintain the joy of the Lord despite painful circumstances).

These are the lessons we learn from Paul and Silas. Paul helped a young woman who was oppressed by the devil by casting out the evil spirit from her. She was making a profit for her masters through soothsaying, and they did not appreciate the loss of income Paul caused. He was arrested and jailed along with his companion, Silas. They were in chains and were placed in the inner chamber of the jail in Philippi. But late that night they began to pray and praise God. The other prisoners heard them. Soon an earthquake broke the prison doors down and the chains fell off the prisoners. The jailer was so shaken by this that he tried to harm himself, but Paul restrained him. The jailer believed in Jesus and took the evangelists to his house in the middle of the night. He washed their wounds and fed them. His entire family was baptized that night.

I made a list of the things that took place that night.

1. Doors opened.
2. Chains fell.

3. The jailer began to shake in fear and was saved.
4. Wounds were washed in the night.
5. Food was served in the night.
6. Family members were saved.
7. Baptisms took place in the night.

This fascinating story is well known. Its implication is that God answers prayers even in the worst of circumstances. However, what needs to be noticed is the two followers of Jesus were able to handle their dire situation with prayer and praise. To me, this is another indication of spiritual growth and maturity.

Followers of Jesus are on a journey of spiritual growth, development, and transformation. This involves the disciples' body, mind, and spirit and affects their knowledge, attitude, values, beliefs, commitments, and behavior. The Word, the Spirit, and the community of faith are involved in this journey called discipleship. For all believers, regardless of their faith community's pneumatology, the involvement of the Holy Spirit is crucial in this journey of faith. Let us now look at the process of spiritual formation that is understood as the continuing work of the Holy Spirit in us.

CHAPTER 4

SPIRITUAL FORMATION AND SANCTIFICATION

> And do not be conformed to this world, but be transformed by the renewing of your mind, that you may prove what is that good and acceptable and perfect will of God. (Rom. 12:2)

Having observed thousands of seminary students and scores of pastors for decades, I am convinced that spiritual knowledge and spiritual formation are not the same. Spiritual formation is more than increased biblical knowledge or cognitive development in spirituality. Formation involves an additional dimension of restorative and transformational grace. I consider it a divine work of grace to put knowledge, attitude, and practice together in a unique, dynamic, and progressive way in the life of disciples in a manner analogous to what systems theorists call second- or third-order change. This represents a change of life that is not just conforming responses to external pressures (external locus of control) but decisions, choices, and a lifestyle governed by internal motivations (internal locus of control) of a transformed person.

Nouwen's Movements

Henri Nouwen was a professor of pastoral care at Yale Divinity School when I was a student there many years ago, and he attempted to describe spiritual formation in terms of what he called movements.[33] He said, "Spiritual formation, I have to believe, is not about steps or stages on the way to perfection. It is about the movements from the mind to the heart through prayer in its many forms that reunite us with God, each other and our truest self."[34] He adapted the word *heart* from the Judeo-Christian tradition that refers to the source of all physical, emotional, intellectual, volitional, and moral energies. This heart is the seat of the will, plans, and decisions. To Nouwen, the heart was the central unifying organ of our life. He listed the seven movements of the Spirit involved in spiritual formation as movements

1. from openness to transparency
2. from illusion to prayer
3. from sorrow to joy
4. from resentment to gratitude
5. from fear to love
6. from exclusion to inclusion
7. from denying death to befriending it

To these he added five spiritual practices to promote spiritual formation:

1. Reflection
2. A form of prayer called *Lectio Divina*

3. Silence
4. Community
5. Service

Nouwen valued silence highly and recommended practicing this discipline regularly. Based on a statement by Seraphim of Sarov, a Russian saint, he believed words are the weapons of this world, but silence is the sacrament of the world to come. He advised Christians to take an inward journey to the heart and an outward journey from the heart to the community for ministry and service to experience spiritual formation. Opening our heart helps us to receive life as a gift rather than an entitlement. When one prays from the heart, the world loses its opaqueness and becomes transparent.[35] Reflective contemplation helps us to see things as they really are and reveals the real connections that make things hang together in the world. According to Nouwen, ordinary time (*chronos*) becomes divine moments (*kairos*) in reflective contemplation.

Nouwen defined prayer as intentional, concentrated, and regular efforts to create space for God in one's life. During prayer, one becomes unbusy with God instead of being busy with other things. Prayer leads one to a lonely place to be with God. Without a lonely place, our lives are in danger, Nouwen believed. In true prayer one descends from the mind to the heart to stand before the face of God, fully present, being able to see within oneself. Theological reflection is the openness of one's mind to God's truth and wisdom, Nouwen taught. Spiritual formation is the grateful openness of one's heart to God and His people. Disciples can abandon themselves to God in prayer when moments become sacraments of joy, gratitude, and loving acceptance of the will of God for one's life. True prayer involves practicing the presence of God. All followers of Jesus need a time and a place of prayer.

Nouwen sees mourning and dancing as part of a continuum. He considers it a movement of grace to move from sorrow to joy. The community is at the heart of the movement from sorrow to joy. Disciples connect their suffering with that of the larger world. One's afflictions are seen in light of the suffering of others. By making the connection between our suffering and God's suffering in Jesus of Nazareth, we can move from sorrow to joy. Nouwen learned these truths from the story of the disciples on the road to Emmaus. He saw five parts to their story:

1. Mourning your losses
2. Connecting your suffering with the great suffering of humanity
3. Inviting the one whom you recognize on the road into your house
4. Entering into communion with Christ living in you
5. Going into the world with joy

"Jesus enters into our sadness, takes us by the hand, pulls us gently up to where we can stand, and invites us to dance," says Nouwen.[36]

Nouwen strongly discouraged bitterness, because it is a retardant to spiritual formation. He believed that resentment only makes us angry with the people and institutions on which we have made ourselves dependent. We are tempted to be like the sons of Zebedee who wanted to be near the power and to reflect the glory. We should try to not cling to our complaints.

Complaints and resentments leave no room for God to enter and bring freedom. Resentment limits the movement of the Spirit and diminishes the kingdom of God within us. Nouwen advised all to replace resentment with gratitude. Resentment prevents us from giving our gifts to others, whereas gratitude sets us free to share, minister, and celebrate.

We can move away from resentment by moving toward an attitude of gratitude, which is lifegiving and frees us to move forward to new possibilities. Spiritual formation is the journey in which resentment is transformed into gratitude. A disciple of Jesus is a grateful person. Resentment, however, is the complaint that life does not unfold the way we planned. One's choice in unplanned situations is not simply to be passive and resentful but to move toward gratitude by realizing that God is the God of history. Life is unfolding under His watch and care. We can trust Him to guide us with His hand to the destiny He has for us. When our work is interrupted, we must consider the possibility that our real work might be the interruptions themselves. Spiritual formation involves listening to God by faith during disruptions.

Gratitude accepts our past as God's way of leading us to the present to take us to the future. We should not be afraid to look back to the way God brought us to the present by lovingly guiding us. Receiving the present with gratitude will help us to launch into our future, still trusting divine guidance. Spiritual formation, to Nouwen, is an ongoing journey as well as the still imperfect outcome.

Spiritual formation is the journey from what Nouwen calls the house of fear to the house of love. When fear takes over our life, we are living in the house of fear. Prayer, however, is the way out of the house of fear to the house of love. Our Christian identity is most valuable in this situation. When we recognize that we are children of God, we will lose our fear. Our true identity is in our belonging in God's family. We must let go of our fear and embrace our true identity as the beloved children of God.

To Nouwen, spiritual formation is the journey from exclusion to inclusion and hospitality is the vital sign of spiritual maturity. Nouwen would agree with Indian Orthodox Church bishop Zachariah Mar Severios Metropolitan, who said that ownership is not the sign of true blessing but relationship and hospitality are. The bishop described the prophet Elijah as a good example of hospitality. He did not own anything. He accepted hospitality from a raven, a widow in Zarephath, and even from a heavenly chariot. The bishop added that the priest and the Levite in the parable of the good Samaritan did not offer hospitality, but the Samaritan did. The philosophy of ownership Jesus taught in this parable is noteworthy: the robber believed that what belonged to the Samaritan was his; the priest and the Levite believed that what was theirs was theirs only; but the Samaritan demonstrated that what was his was also the victim's. This is hospitality.

Hospitality is inclusive. It opens space in the soul for a wide range of positive experiences. By being inclusive and hospitable, Abraham entertained angels without knowing it. To Nouwen, ministry is hospitality. An authentic minister offers the gifts of inclusion, availability, and hospitality. This reminds me of the story of a priest who, after formally refusing to give permission to bury a Protestant in a Catholic cemetery because of a policy, allowed the burial just outside the fence of the cemetery, and then moved the fence in the night to include the fresh grave. Hospitality makes room for others, especially the weak.

Hospitality and availability can be practiced in powerful ways. Hospitality allows us to accept people as they are. We can be with people who are not at all like us and be with them in personal, compassionate, and creative ways. Instead of judging and comparing, we can accept, affirm, and celebrate others. Within such a relationship, a guest can see Christian love, hear the good news, and choose to become a follower of Christ. According to Nouwen, God's plan for us is to live this way and become the body of Christ by eating and drinking together in the circle of God's love. He believes this is where one is really transformed.

The God of all the nations is not our private God. Intimacy with God must coexist with solidarity with others in a true disciple's heart. Spiritual formation is not a one-dimensional exercise. The vertical and the horizontal relationships demonstrate the active presence of God in our lives.

Christians should not live in fear of illness, death, and the future. Such fears allow society to manipulate us with threats and promises, forcing us to conform to this world. Our fear of death disappears when we can believe we were loved before we were born and we will be loved after we die. When this fear is gone, we can realize God's plan for our lives and fulfill our mission during our life. I recall a comforting thought while meeting with a bereaving family at the City of Faith Hospital in Tulsa—there is no need for a Christian to fear death, because as one's birth goes on as God planned without much worry or work on one's part, so will go one's death. Followers of Jesus will make the passage from this life to the next, through death, under the caring watch of the loving heavenly Father and will find themselves delightfully surprised on the other side of this existence just as they arrived in this world through birth.

In Nouwen's case, he did not want to be alone at the time of his death and hoped for someone to be with him as a midwife into death. He testified of having an immense sense of security and freedom regarding his death. He is now gone and was not alone when he departed, as he had wished. I remember him as a revered professor and listener at Yale Divinity School during my sojourn there. I witnessed his hospitality to so many students who lined up at his office door at Yale.

Nouwen presented a nonhierarchical, nonsystematic, integrative, and pastorally sensitive model of spiritual formation. He left a nonprescriptive map of spiritual journey that was not a pursuit of perfection. Instead, it involves prayer, community, and mission. It involves following the movement of the Spirit in our hearts, which is discerned through prayer and reflection, not by some step-by-step instruction book. Nouwen believed that when our heart is open to the Spirit, healthy movements will occur, and spiritual formation will result unexpectedly and in ways unforeseen.

Willard's Manifesto

The book *The Kingdom Life*[37] was written by several Protestant colleagues to provide a practical theology of discipleship and spiritual formation. This book is considered an evangelical manifesto on spiritual formation. These authors have broken the multiple elements of spiritual formation into two categories: process elements and theological elements. I will try to summarize the major contributions of these writers without going into the multitude of elements. Spiritual formation is rooted in relationship with God and with one another in the body of Christ. It is in our communities of grace that we discover and define who we are and how we shall live. Life must be lived in trust, love, grace, humility, dignity, and justice. Spiritual formation involves an intentional public, personal, and communal commitment to living as disciples of Jesus with the awareness that we are being transformed into His image in all aspects of our life.

Spiritual formation is a lifelong journey in pursuit of being conformed to the image of Jesus Christ. This is not a matter of external activity alone, but it is a matter of the heart. Spiritual formation must involve the whole person. It is not just the application of certain techniques or programs to deal with only some aspects of our life. The biblical images of spiritual formation represent efforts of long duration, such as training for a race, wandering through the wilderness, etc. Spiritual formation is not a matter of quick fixes based on established techniques and using the right tools and programs. It is a process of learning, growing, and transforming, a process of growing in kingdom living and participating in God's mission in the world. Spiritual formation is not a self-help process but has to do with the advancement of the kingdom of God.

The theology of spiritual transformation is rooted in the trinitarian nature of God—relational, loving, gracious, mutually submissive, and unified in will. It is the indwelling Holy Spirit who empowers disciples for a life of faith and mission both in the church and in the world. The Bible is the guidebook of spiritual formation.

The contemporary church, with its consumer mentality, is not sufficiently invested in the process of making disciples and is failing in leading people to grow spiritually and be formed into the image of Christ, say the many authors of *The Kingdom Life*. The church is focused on the best techniques for the fastest results, but this is not the way to promote spiritual formation. We must recognize there are principalities and powers at work within the systems of our culture, and by allowing them to invade the church or permitting them to be imitated in the church works against the purposes of the church in terms of making disciples who are formed in the image of Christ. Discipleship and spiritual formation are not simply self-improvement programs. These involve the work of grace in our lives, doing that which only God through His Spirit can do.

Disciples are called to live with Jesus and to learn to live a kingdom lifestyle, as He did. One can live this way only by grace, which is God working in our lives to accomplish what only He can accomplish. Life in the kingdom is a gift of God, and spiritual formation is our response to this gift. This life is in opposition to the control of the trinity of evil—the world, the flesh, and the devil (Eph. 2:1–2).

The authors of *The Kingdom Life* call believers to get past what Dallas Willard calls "sin management theology." This theology reduces godliness to a formula, he says. Seeing godliness as the net gain between more right behavior and less wrong behavior is a formula to fail. When one is born again, God gives us the DNA of godliness. It is important to incorporate the new identity and live out of that identity. There should not be two classes of Christians, such as converted Christians and disciples. All Christians are called to discipleship. Even "entry-level" Christians are disciples of Jesus. In this perspective, Willard and his fellow authors are on the same page as A. W. Tozer.

We must learn who we are from our community of faith. We need to believe who we are as God tells us, instead of creating an identity based on what we think we should become. Mistaken identity prevents true spiritual formation. Traditionally, the question has been, If you were to die tonight, would you go to heaven? But the question should be, If you know you are going to live forever, what kind of person would you like to become? The first question focuses on a crisis event. The second focuses on a process. Spiritual formation is a process, not an event.

Disciples are apprentices of Jesus. A missional gospel model or a conversion-focused model does not fulfill the biblical mandate to make disciples. Discipleship first is apprenticeship. Seeking Christlikeness must become the heart of the gospel. While spiritual disciplines are important, and they can produce change, what would Jesus do is not the sure path to Christlikeness. Discipleship should be deeper than behavior modification.

Again, the community is a vital aspect of spiritual formation. Community is a concept grounded in the trinitarian nature of God. Even the apostle Paul submitted himself to a community of disciples and followers of Jesus in Jerusalem.

Within the community of faith individuals are transformed. The community of faith acts as a mirror, reflecting the grace of God to us and at the same time shining our lives back to us. In spiritual formation, we join a process that was already operating before we joined the race.

Spiritual formation is a lifelong process of sanctification involving learning and change. The journey to conform to the character of Jesus cannot be accomplished in a hurry. The purpose of discipleship is for each follower of Jesus to be like Him. The goal is the same for all followers, regardless of their place in the church or society. God is the source of strength for all to accomplish this goal.

Spiritual formation is not limited to internal matters. God works from inside out and outside in. Transformation begins in the mind of the disciple and renews the mind. Paul's words are vital here: "Do not conform to the pattern of this world, but be transformed by the renewing of your mind. Then you will be able to test and approve what God's will is—his good, pleasing and perfect will" (Rom. 12:2 NIV). This is the same idea Paul shared with the Philippians: "Therefore, my dear friends, as you have always obeyed—not only in my presence, but now much more in my absence—continue to work out your salvation with fear and trembling, for it is God who works in you to will and to act in order to fulfill his good purpose" (Phil. 2:12–13 NIV).

There is a clear distinction between discipleship and spiritual formation. Discipleship has to do with the decision to follow Jesus. It is a matter of positioning ourselves as followers, making ourselves available to change. Spiritual formation, on the other hand, is the direct operation of the Holy Spirit on the one who follows. The Word of God is at work in disciples to transform them. God's Word reveals secrets to disciples, even things unknown to them about themselves.

There is no transformation of life without a meaningful interaction with the Word of God. Spiritual formation also involves the heart of the disciple. Like Nouwen, Willard and his colleagues define the heart as the inner center of a person where body, mind, and spirit blend. The heart can move toward God or away from Him. A true disciple develops a heart for God. Thus, spiritual formation involves the Word, Spirit, and the community of faith in the changing body, mind, and spirit. The Word and the Spirit work on the disciples within the community and transform their heart.

We are saved by faith, not by works, but an effort in spiritual life is a good thing. Paul worked, pressed forward, and struggled. Faith involves work. Faith acts. "What good is it, my brothers and sisters, if someone claims to have faith but has no deeds? Can such faith save them? Suppose a brother or a sister is without clothes and daily food. If one of you says to them, 'Go in peace; keep warm and well fed,' but does nothing about their physical needs, what good is it? In the same way, faith by itself, if it is not accompanied by action, is dead" (James 2:14–17 NIV). Faith must lead to action. So using traditional spiritual disciplines for spiritual formation is acceptable. These tools can help to train the heart of the disciple. Structured discipleship programs involving activities and curriculums help disciples to grow in grace. However, these should not be used in a utilitarian fashion with modern church-growth philosophies. Spiritual formation is more important than institutional expansion and survival. It is also more than therapeutic pastoral counseling. A new way is needed to implement ministries that promote spiritual formation and produce whole life transformation.

A new emphasis on more relevant biblical metaphors is needed to accomplish this. Not organizational relationships, but "organic" relationships like coaching are needed. Self-help sermons and motivational worship will not fix the problem at hand. Paul's metaphors of agriculture, military, and journey must be rediscovered in our postmodern world.

Dallas Willard and his colleagues expressed concern for the American paradigm of personal salvation. They believe it is not compatible with the words of Jesus instructing a lawyer: "'You shall love the LORD your God with all your heart, with all your soul, with all your strength, and with all your mind,' and 'your neighbor as yourself'" (Luke 10:27). Loving the neighbor must also be a factor in any effort to disciple people and lead them to spiritual maturity. The gospel must be more than an entry into the future heaven; it must touch someone and their current environment because the gospel is the good news for today and for eternity.

Spirit and Spiritual Formation

The work of the Holy Spirit is essential to the process of spiritual formation. As mentioned earlier, many Christians are binitarians when it comes to their relationship with the Holy Spirit. They confess faith in a trinitarian God but live as if only the Father and the Son are involved in their life of faith. One must remain open to the ongoing work of the Holy Spirit to undergo true change and transformation. "We are called to share in the community life of the godhead," says Dallas Willard. We receive the life-giving energy of the Holy Spirit and are transformed. God the creator and Christ the sustainer and the empowering Holy Spirit apply the benefits of salvation to those who trust Christ. Transformation is not just a solo enterprise. It is the work of God the Father, God the Son, and God the Holy Spirit in a believer's life. We are the children of the Father and are being transformed into the likeness of the Son by the power of the Holy Spirit.

Sacraments have a role to play in a disciple's spiritual formation. Participating in the ordinances of the church impacts the disciple in a transformational way. Like the exercise of spiritual disciplines, participation in the ordinances of the church enhances one's life in Christ.

Yet the role of the Holy Spirit is discounted in many Christian circles. We must remember that after the day of pentecost the work of the Holy Spirit was emphasized as the Spirit applied the benefits of the work of the Son in the body of Christ. The work of the Holy Spirit is actually fourfold: conviction and repentance, faith generation and indwelling, sealing and assurance, and holiness and sanctification.

The Bible is vital to the transformational work of the Spirit. Disciples are not to worship the Bible, but they should worship the God who has revealed Himself through the Bible. "All Scripture is given by inspiration of God, and is profitable for doctrine, for reproof, for correction, for instruction in righteousness, that the man of God may be complete, thoroughly equipped for every good work" (2 Tim. 3:16–17).

Both the Old and New Testaments should be treated as a script for our lives as we follow the guidance of the Holy Spirit. The Bible is both descriptive and prescriptive. Daily life in obedience to Christ requires daily dwelling on the Word of God. Meditating on Scripture passages is a very important habit for the disciple. Prayerful reading and study of the Bible promotes spiritual formation as God's Spirit illuminates His Word to us. The Bible must be read spiritually, not just intellectually, to help spiritual formation. A disciple must be a serious student of the Bible, reading the Scripture regularly and learning to interpret biblical passages intelligently and spiritually. The Bible needs to be read for information and for transformation. Informational reading and spiritual reading should complement each other. This involves digging into what a passage means and stopping from time to time to meditate on the implications of the passage and its impact on our life.

The Bible must become the primary textbook for spiritual formation, says Dallas Willard. All other resources, including classical texts from various traditions, should be evaluated based on the Bible. In a Bible-based method of spiritual formation, we will have Jesus Christ and His kingdom as its center. Spiritual formation is three dimensional as it involves engagement in personal, community, and missional formation.

A biblically sound spiritual formation effort requires an environment of grace that welcomes everyone. Through preaching, teaching, and engagement in practical life with the Spirit, a church can be a center for spiritual formation. Equipping people for the work of ministry is also critical to this process. However, this cannot be just programs and activities of an organization called the church. Biblical metaphors to describe the church as the people of God are not organizational. They are primarily organic, such as body, sheep, and family. The vision of the church as an organism must be recaptured.

Rabbis, Jesus, and Paul

Greg Ogden's *Transforming Discipleship* presents two models of discipleship: Jesus' model of discipleship and Paul's approach to discipleship. Before discussing Jesus' model of disciple making, let us take a brief look at the history of discipleship itself. Although the term *discipleship* is not found in the Old Testament, the concept of teaching, training, and mentoring individuals for service in the community is amply documented in the Hebrew Scriptures. The concept is related to the transmission of God's Word from one generation to the next. Moses and Joshua, Eli and Samuel, and Elijah and Elisha are examples of generational mentoring. We read about schools of the prophets where "formational" work obviously took place. Rabbis who received instruction from their elders passed on their heritage to those who followed them. Often this involved passing on the knowledge of God through oral tradition.

The Old Testament emphasizes the parents' duty to train their children in the things of God. This was a non-negotiable responsibility, as we can see in the instruction Joshua gave to all the tribes before they crossed Jordan to enter the promised land:

> Cross over before the ark of the Lord your God into the midst of the Jordan, and each one of you take up a

> stone on his shoulder, according to the number of the tribes of the children of Israel, that this may be a sign among you when your children ask in time to come, saying, "What do these stones mean to you?" Then you shall answer them that the waters of the Jordan were cut off before the ark of the covenant of the LORD; when it crossed over the Jordan, the waters of the Jordan were cut off. And these stones shall be for a memorial to the children of Israel forever. (Josh. 4:5–7)

What we see in the leaders and prophets is the additional training built on this early "education" given to a select group of people.

According to Hindu tradition, the idea of Gurukula (place of learning from a Guru or Master) existed as early as 800 BC. There is evidence that by 400 BC Greek philosophers and teachers had disciples. It is believed this practice of "educating and training" seekers of knowledge spread throughout the Greek world. Both Socrates and his disciple Plato had disciples.

Jewish rabbis were experts in teaching the Torah to develop moral disciplines and values in their novices. The rabbis were well versed in the Torah, and they encouraged their pupils to memorize the texts they studied. Jewish discipleship flourished during the intertestamental period.

By the time of Jesus, discipleship was a common practice among the Jews in terms of the rabbi-learner relationship. The rabbis spent years with their disciples, teaching the Torah, giving training in the Jewish way of life, and modeling how to teach the Scripture. One major difference between Jesus and

His contemporaries seems to be the process of initiating the relationship with potential disciples. Often potential disciples sought the rabbis. Jesus, however, initiated the relationship by calling His disciples. Indeed, He called some unlikely candidates for His unprecedented mission.

In Jesus' model, disciples join His life first, then join His community, and ultimately join His mission. Jesus did not try to reach as many as possible. He preferred to focus on a few selected ones. Jesus' legacy was preserved not through His writings or the crowds He addressed, but through the Holy Spirit and His twelve disciples. According to Greg Ogden, the mistake of the modern church is its effort to reach the masses through mass means instead of training a smaller group of disciples whom the masses could emulate. Jesus' model of discipleship could be called an empowerment model. In His model, the person of the disciple maker becomes the vehicle for transmission of His life to these disciples. For Jesus, discipleship centered on Him, His person. Knowing Him and loving Him were keys to spiritual transformation. Jesus' vision was so large that He could think small, Ogden observes.

Jesus chose the most unlikely candidates for discipleship. Uneducated people of humble birth and low social status with mean occupations were selected. Eleven of the twelve were from the hill country of Galilee. Their speech betrayed their low social status. Jesus was able to adapt His discipleship style to the readiness level of His candidates. We may call this a situational leadership model. The apostle Paul used the same leadership approach, but his model of discipleship was different, according to Ogden.

Paul's model of discipleship used a different vocabulary to describe the process of spiritual formation. Paul never spoke about having disciples. Instead, he presented the image of parenting. The purpose of discipleship for Paul was to help believers mature in Christ. Paul's primary goal for Christians was to reach a state of maturity. Ogden believes that Paul had a post-pentecost perspective on the indwelling presence of the Holy Spirit. To Paul, Christian life begins at spiritual infancy, and it has the potential to reach the full measure of the stature of Christ. Paul uses phrases such as "put on" and "put off," "be transformed," "renew the mind," etc. Listen to his words to the Corinthians and Ephesians:

> And I, brethren, could not speak to you as to spiritual people but as to carnal, as to babes in Christ. I fed you with milk and not with solid food; for until now you were not able to receive it, and even now you are still not able. (1 Cor. 3:1–2)
>
> Brethren, do not be children in understanding; however, in malice be babes, but in understanding be mature. (1 Cor. 14:20)
>
> And He Himself gave some to be apostles, some prophets, some evangelists, and some pastors and teachers, for the equipping of the saints for the work of ministry, for the edifying of the body of Christ, till we all come to the unity of the faith and of the knowledge of the Son of God, to a perfect man, to the measure of the stature of the fullness of Christ; that we should no longer be children, tossed to and from and carried

> about with every wind of doctrine, by the trickery of men, in the cunning craftiness of deceitful plotting, but, speaking the truth in love, may grow up in all things into Him who is the head—Christ. (Eph. 4:11–15)

To Paul, discipleship involves an intentional journey to become a truly spiritual person. Spiritual formation is a lifelong journey in pursuit of being conformed to the image of Jesus Christ. Paul's model of discipleship and spiritual formation takes a believer from a state of conformity to the world to a transformed life. It is a movement from conformation to transformation. It takes a person from infancy to maturity in Christ. Maturity is the disciples' readiness to have the nature of Jesus reflect through every aspect of their being. Paul's desire was to see believers being transformed as Christ was formed in them. Paul imagined God staring into our lives to see if Christ is formed in us.

Paul's understanding of his role as an apostle in the lives of his converts affirms this concept of spiritual formation. The disciple maker is a nurse and the nursing mother: "But we were gentle among you, just as a nursing mother cherishes her own children. So, affectionately longing for you, we were well pleased to impart to you not only the gospel of God, but also our own lives, because you had become dear to us" (1 Thess. 2:7–8). Like a father, the disciple maker urges, encourages, and pleads with the new believer: "You are witnesses, and God also, how devoutly and justly and blamelessly we behaved ourselves among you who believe; as you know how we exhorted, and comforted, and charged every one of you, as a father does his own children, that you would walk worthy of God who calls you into His own kingdom and glory" (1 Thess. 2:10–12).

According to Paul, the disciple maker loves these disciples with true agape, watching them walk worthy of God by being transformed by the renewing of their mind. The disciple maker is also a coach, not just a teacher. Coaching is formational work, not just instruction or passing on information. Paul called Timothy "my beloved son" and "a beloved son" (2 Tim. 1:2). Similar language is noteworthy elsewhere in Paul's writings.

> Therefore, my beloved and longed-for brethren, my joy and crown, so stand fast in the Lord, beloved. (Phil. 4:1)
>
> Therefore, my beloved, flee from idolatry. (1 Cor. 10:14)
>
> Likewise greet the church that is in their house. Greet my beloved Epaenetus, who is the firstfruits of Achaia to Christ. (Rom. 16:5)

In Paul's model, according to Greg Ogden, there is no hierarchy. The disciple maker is not above the disciple. The relationship is a partnership built on collegiality and friendship. Paul was a coworker with those whom he was discipling. Philemon was his friend and coworker: "To Philemon our beloved friend and fellow laborer" (Philem. 1:1).

Ogden believes Paul mirrored Jesus' situational leadership model, but Paul used a different vocabulary where the focus of discipleship is on relationship. Relationships provide intimacy, responsibility, and accountability. Discipleship to Paul was a longer process. It was customized to the individual. According to Ogden, discipleship is an intentional relationship in which we walk alongside other disciples to encourage, equip, and challenge one another in love to grow toward maturity in Christ. This includes equipping the disciples to teach others too. Spiritual formation involves moving toward spiritual maturity as well as spiritual productiveness. Disciple makers train their trainees to reproduce.

Ogden finds the Paul-Timothy model insufficient as it assumes the relationship involved to be between an older person and a younger person, like a parent-child relationship or teacher-student relationship. He also sees a hierarchy in the relationship where one is spiritually more mature with more experience and authority. There are some unwelcome consequences to this definition of relationship. The disciple maker carries the responsibility, promotes dependence, limits dialogue, and assumes that one model applies to everyone. Additionally, there is no emphasis on reproduction. Ogden recommends moving from a Paul-Timothy model to a Barnabas-Paul model, as it promises empowering of the disciple and multiplication through peer mentoring.

Personally, I endorse both the Paul-Timothy and the Barnabas-Paul models. I believe the so-called power difference is not necessarily a liability within covenant relationships. Maturity and experience should not be disqualifiers for disciple makers. The context should be the main consideration, not hierarchy. Disciple making should happen in contextually appropriate ways.

CHAPTER 5

LEGALISM VERSUS BIBLICAL SPIRITUALITY

There is therefore now no condemnation to those who are in Christ Jesus, who do not walk according to the flesh, but according to the Spirit. (Rom. 8:1)

What is your highest spiritual goal? Is it just to keep all the religious rules of your faith group? Or do you want to live a transformed life? In other words, do you wish to be a disciple of Jesus Christ, who lives as if you are already seated in heavenly places with Christ? What do I mean? Let me share with you what the apostle Paul told both the Ephesian and Colossian followers of Jesus about such a life. You may remember that Paul met about twelve followers of John the Baptist who had not heard about the Holy Spirit. He baptized them in the name of Jesus and prayed for them to be empowered by the Holy Spirit. They received the Holy Spirit and probably were pioneer members of the church in

Ephesus (Acts 19:1–7). To that church, Paul wrote these words: "But God, who is rich in mercy, because of His great love with which He loved us, even when we were dead in trespasses, made us alive together with Christ (by grace you have been saved), and raised us up together, and made us sit together in the heavenly places in Christ Jesus" (Eph. 2:4–6). He sent a similar message to the Colossians: "If then you were raised with Christ, seek those things which are above, where Christ is, sitting at the right hand of God. Set your mind on things above, not on things on the earth. For you died, and your life is hidden with Christ in God" (Col. 3:1–3). To me, these passages describe a nonlegalistic, Spirit-empowered, liberating spirituality a disciple is called to live.

The postmodern period in which we live has defined its own spirituality, and many Christians have adopted it without scrutinizing it from a biblical perspective. Our secular culture has adapted a Christian vocabulary but given new meanings to words that are totally opposite to their original meanings. Now many do not want any type of religion, because they have separated spirituality from any religious faith and only prefer spirituality as it is defined by cultural icons, not sacred texts. Tolerance is their highest value, so the postmodernists have come up with mind-blowing models of spirituality where all religions are equal, all religious leaders are equal, and all religious texts are equally authoritative.

I was surprised when my students at the premier pentecostal-charismatic seminary in the world (Oral Roberts University) could not define Spirit-led or Spirit-empowered spirituality. Ironically, they could define the spiritualities of other religions based on at least some of their practices. For instance, concerning Hindu spirituality, they identified these markers: the repetition of mantras, the puja or ceremonial invocation, dietary practices, worshipping the sun, moon, stars, air, earth, water, birds, fishes, animals, and all the elements and forces of Mother Nature. Regarding Buddhist spirituality and practices, my students mentioned the following: meditation called zazen, meditation on paradoxes to empty the self (a nonself), writing poetry called haiku, tea ceremonies, painting, and maintenance of Zen gardens. My students also had ideas about Muslim spirituality. They noted the five pillars of Islam: (1) Shahada or profession of faith, (2) Salat or ritual washing and prayer, (3) Zakah or almsgiving, (4) Sawm or fasting during Ramdan, and (5) the Hajj or pilgrimage to Mecca.

Steve Land's Trio

To assist them, I introduced the class to my friend Steve Land, the former president of the Pentecostal Theological Seminary (previously Church of God Theological Seminary), who did considerable research on this subject. According to Land, there are three dimensions to Spirit-filled Christian spirituality: orthodoxy, orthopathy, and orthopraxy. In other words, right doctrines, right affections, and right practices. Orthodoxy, or doctrinal purity, is important to Spirit-empowered spirituality. What a disciple believes must be biblically sound theology. There are people who believe that theology is not important, and they are wrong. Others claim they do not have a theology at all. That is not true. Everyone has a theology. Some have bad theology while others have good theology. The quality of the theology is the issue. I recall a medical doctor telling me about bad theology when I was a chaplain at the City of Faith Hospital in Tulsa, Oklahoma. He said, "Bad medicine kills, but so does bad theology." We must learn from the Bereans mentioned in the book of Acts and evaluate everything in the light of the Word of God: "These were more fair-minded than those in Thessalonica, in that they received the word with all readiness, and searched the Scriptures daily to find out whether these things were so" (Acts 17:11). When confronted with a false teaching, a disciple should ask, "Where in the Word did you get this?"

Healthy spirituality has orthopathy, or affections. According to Land, there are three affections: compassion (for the needy), courage (to go where the good news is not known), and gratitude to God (that leads to spiritual worship). All followers of Jesus should exemplify these affections. Land said the overarching affection is the kingdom of God. In other words, all affections are guided by the claims of the kingdom of God rather than personal needs.

Although there are many exceptions, I must sadly say that genuine Spirit-empowered spirituality is on the decline today, especially in the pentecostal-charismatic movement. The main backsliding has been in the area of affections. If gratitude, compassion, courage, and the kingdom of God were formerly the main religious affections, today the following "affections" seem to be more highly regarded: entitlement, competition, security, and personal kingdom. Entitlement rather than gratitude. Competition rather than compassion. Security rather than courage. And personal kingdom rather than the kingdom of God.

Gathered together regularly to express their profound gratitude to God for their salvation and all the provisions He gave to a marginalized people, the pioneer pentecostals fasted, prayed, sang, and testified. Regardless of distance and the lack of comfortable transportation, they gathered together with others of their like precious faith as often as possible. They were simply grateful. It appears that gratitude has been replaced by a sense of entitlement. It is the mindset of the prodigal son before he left home. The father owed the son, he claimed. He was entitled to his inheritance. He did not have to be grateful. So worship has to be pumped out from congregations now by pastors. Praise must be squeezed out by worship leaders. Singing at conventions and conferences has been delegated to highly paid music groups. The professional singers are no longer just worship leaders; they do the worship for the worshippers!

Competition has replaced compassion. Evangelism used to be based on love for the lost. Now it is a matter of who is in charge. One group wants to be larger and louder than another, willing to duplicate any ineffective efforts at a higher cost just to keep up with the Joneses. It is all about one's group identity and brand.

Courage has become another casualty. The pioneers had the courage to witness to a hostile culture. They were a deprived and abused people, but they had the courage to stand up for what they believed. It was not about politics and elections and sloganeering. It was all about having convictions and the courage to stand up for them. Their personal security was not their main concern, and preachers did not walk around with bodyguards.

Additionally, in many circles, ministry now has become a matter of building personal kingdoms. Nothing much is said about the kingdom of God. It is about "my ministry," not "His ministry." Self-promotion is the mode of operation, social media is the field, and gospel stardom is the goal. Leaders are everywhere, servants are few. Ministries are everywhere, ministers are few. Crusades are everywhere, converts are few. Dignitaries are everywhere, disciples are few!

Spiritual practices (orthopraxy) are also part of true Spirit-led spirituality. These are more than the spiritual practices evangelicals are familiar with. The Bible gives several lists of spiritual practices. Such practices in the first church in Jerusalem are listed in Acts 2. They included studying the apostle's doctrines, fellowship, breaking bread, prayers, joyful worship, signs and wonders, sharing possessions, and sharing the faith with others (vv. 42–47). Paul gave a short list to the Thessalonians: (1) rejoice evermore, (2) pray without ceasing, (3) in everything give thanks, and (4) quench not the Spirit. Despite these and similar lists, Spirit-empowered spirituality is not about fulfilling a list of dos and don'ts (1 Thess. 5:16–19).

Spirit-empowered spiritual practices are more than preferable activities focused only on external appearances. Spiritual disciplines must always be a part of the disciple's life, but true spirituality must be seen as expressions of the work of the Holy Spirit inside a believer simply manifesting on the outside. Legalism flourishes where checklists are longer. In some circles, the checklists keep growing and changing. Many young Christians have left the faith in despair because they could not fulfill the legalists' ever-changing pharisaical demands. Legalism is a threat to true discipleship as its focus is conformity to external expectations, not development of disciplines and spiritual expressions of changed lives.

A disciple is supposed to live a changed life, not a perfect life. We should be able to do that from the first moment after our new birth, because the Bible says we are changed instantly by the power of the Spirit of Christ. We do not mature instantly, but we are changed instantly. We do not become spiritual giants overnight, but we are changed supernaturally and set on a course to spiritual growth and maturity. The change happens not after our physical death but here and now, following our new birth. We are seated in heavenly places now, by faith, and our life must demonstrate that truth.

This is Paul's message to the believers in Corinth, Galatia, Ephesus, Colossae, and other places:

> And such were some of you. But you were washed, but you were sanctified, but you were justified in the name of the Lord Jesus and by the Spirit of our God. (1 Cor. 6:11)
>
> I have been crucified with Christ; it is no longer I who live, but Christ lives in me; and the life which I now live in the flesh I live by faith in the Son of God, who loved me and gave Himself for me. (Gal. 2:20)
>
> This I say, therefore, and testify in the Lord, that you should no longer walk as the rest of the Gentiles walk, in the futility of their mind. (Eph. 4:17)
>
> For you died, and your life is hidden with Christ in God. (Col. 3:3)

Paul explained the process of change to the Ephesians:

> And you He made alive, who were dead in trespasses and sins, in which you once walked according to the course of this world, according to the prince of the power of the air, the spirit who now works in the sons of disobedience, among whom also we all once conducted ourselves in the lusts of our flesh, fulfilling the desires of the flesh and of the mind, and were by nature children of wrath, just as the others.
>
> But God, who is rich in mercy, because of His great love with which He loved us, even when we were dead in trespasses, made us alive together with Christ (by grace you have been saved), and raised us up together, and made us sit together in the heavenly places in Christ Jesus, that in the ages to come He might show the exceeding riches of His grace in His kindness toward us in Christ Jesus. (2:1–7)

We are not only adopted by God to be His children, but we also are born again and born of the Spirit. That means we have a new spiritual DNA that enables us to live a new spirituality (lifestyle). In the past, we were dead in our trespasses and sin. We were aliens, living outside the covenant of faith, with no hope and without God, but our present is completely transformed. Now we are accepted, adopted, forgiven, crucified, raised, a masterpiece of God, sealed by the Holy Spirit, rich in inheritance, citizens of heaven, members of the household of faith, and seated in heavenly places, *now*! By faith, our present already is very much like our future.

Born of the Spirit: A New DNA

All this is possible because of the love of God the Father who sent His Son into the world. Paul's letter to the Ephesians describes the church of Jesus Christ and his epistle to the Colossians describes the Christ of the church. Ephesians describes the body of Christ. Colossians describes the head of the body—Jesus Christ. All the fullness of the Godhead is in Jesus, Paul taught. He is seated at the right hand of the Father, and we are seated with Him in heavenly places *now*! While on earth, we live in Him, we are rooted in Him, we are hidden in Him, and we are alive in Him. As J. W. Phillips wrote in his Pursuing with Passion series,[38] we are children of God now, not through genetics as Jews, not through self-improvement exercises or through long-term spiritual therapy, but through grafting. God has grafted us to His vine, His nature. We receive divine life and nature from Him, not from our biological or religious family. God initiated this process and continues to provide the energy for us to live this out. This is the essence of Spirit-empowered spirituality. This should be the spirituality of a true disciple of Jesus.

Again, a disciple has the DNA to live such a life without great distress. Phillips stated, as lion babies have the nature of lions and bear babies have the nature of bears, God's babies should have His nature. It does not have to be manufactured. One inherits this nature. The unsaved are called sinners. The saved ones are not called sinners but saints. We are saints now, according to the Bible, even those of us who are not fully mature yet. Our old nature was wicked (Jer. 17:9). Our righteousness was like filthy rags (Isa. 64:6). We could not repair ourselves, but God made us a new creation in Christ.

Born of God and brought to life in Christ by His Spirit, our life is now hidden in Christ. We have been set free and changed. We are God's workmanship, His masterpiece (Col. 3:3; Eph. 2:10). Although legalism hides this, this is a profound truth! If God's Word—"Let there be . . ."—created the real universe, our new birth by His word must also be real.

This is a very different way of looking at discipleship and spiritual formation. This works against performance-based churches and sin management–based discipleship programs. Disciples of Jesus must live this lifestyle by faith and by dependence on the Holy Spirit. They must live in the assurance of this just as formerly enslaved African Americans had to claim their freedom after the pronouncement of Abraham Lincoln's Emancipation Proclamation. The enslaved had to hear the message, believe the message, reckon for themselves the truth of the message, act on it, and assert it, knowing the whole weight of the federal government stood behind the proclamation.

Spiritual formation is a gradual process. Maturity is only slowly achieved, but according to the Bible, the change of life is *now*, the victory is *now*, and the holiness is *now*. This is the truth underlying nonlegalistic, liberating, Spirit-empowered spirituality. The disciples of Jesus recognize they have been crucified and are now a new creation. They belong to the kingdom of God. They live now by faith in the Son of God who loved them and gave Himself for them! The Holy Spirit who has sealed them is empowering them to live this new life. They know the Spirit that raised Jesus from the dead dwells in them. He has transformed them and is transforming them. They simply must keep walking in step with the Spirit.

CHAPTER 6

GOD'S CALL, DISCIPLESHIP, AND VOCATIONAL MINISTRY

Follow Me, and I will make you fishers of men.
(Matt. 4:19)

God's call is a major theme in the Bible. Everything about the journey of faith for a Christian begins with a call. If the gospel in one verse is John 3:16—"For God so loved the world that He gave His only begotten Son, that whoever believes in Him should not perish but have everlasting life"—then the gospel in one word is "come": come and follow (Mark 1:17), "come and eat" (John 21:12), "come and see" (John 1:39). It is an invitation, a call to follow.

> "Come, follow me," Jesus said, "and I will send you out to fish for people." (Matt. 4:19 NIV)
>
> Follow me, and let the dead bury their own dead. (Matt. 8:22 NIV)

> Then Jesus said to his disciples, "Whoever wants to be my disciple must deny themselves and take up their cross and follow me." (Matt. 16:24 NIV)

Discipleship is our life as we follow Jesus; Christian ministry is the overflow of our life as disciples of Jesus.

All of us are called to ministry. The ultimate purpose of discipleship and ministry is to produce disciples and ministers. Paul makes it clear that the purpose of ministry is to enable believers to grow in Christ and equip them to do the work of the ministry.

> And He Himself gave some to be apostles, some prophets, some evangelists, and some pastors and teachers, for the equipping of the saints for the work of ministry, for the edifying of the body of Christ, till we all come to the unity of the faith and of the knowledge of the Son of God, to a perfect man, to the measure of the stature of the fullness of Christ. (Eph. 4:11–13)

Call and Vocation

While all disciples of Jesus are called to become ministers as disciple makers, some are called to serve God through vocational ministry. In his book *The Purpose of the Church and Its Ministry*, Protestant theologian Richard Niebuhr outlines four distinct calls one will experience in discovering God's specific call for a vocation in ministry.[39] The first is the call to become a Christian. Everyone receives this call, but the future minister receives an additional secret call. This is one's inner sense of a calling that is not shared by anyone else. This secret call is followed by a providential call that voluntarily manifests itself through God-given gifts and talents. Finally, ministers receive what Niebuhr calls an ecclesiastical call that publicly acknowledges God's call on their life. In this stage, God's call is publicly affirmed by the body of Christ and may be confirmed through ordination.

The Bible clearly illustrates that an encounter with God is a prerequisite for authentic life and service to God. Abraham, the father of all who believe, had an encounter with the living God (Gen. 17:1–6). Similarly, Moses experienced a powerful encounter with God before he was commissioned (Ex. 3:1–7). Moses trained Joshua, but prior to the commencement of Joshua's leadership, he also had an encounter with God:

> After the death of Moses the servant of the Lord, it came to pass that the Lord spoke to Joshua the son of Nun, Moses' assistant, saying: "Moses My servant is dead. Now therefore, arise, go over this Jordan, you and all this people, to the land which I am giving to them—the children of Israel. . . . As I was with Moses, so I will be with you; I will not leave you nor forsake you." (Josh. 1:1–2, 5)

Samuel, the great Old Testament prophet, had an encounter with God while he was still a child (1 Sam. 3:4). He heard God's voice when the sons of Eli the priest did not. The Word of the Lord came down to Elijah (1 Kings 17:2) and launched him into a great ministry of service to God and His people. Elisha also heard the Lord (2 Kings 7:1). Isaiah encountered God in the year King Uzziah died (Isa. 6:1). He had a glimpse of God's holiness, which confronted his own inadequacies, causing him to cry out, "Woe is me" (v. 5). Isaiah experienced the touch of God's fire and responded to His call, "Whom shall I send, and who will go for Us?" (v. 8).

Individual encounters with the divine continued to occur in the New Testament period as a prerequisite of ministry. Saul of Tarsus, for example, encountered the living Savior and experienced a transformed life; the persecutor became a preacher of the gospel.

An encounter with God that gives a sense of calling is a definite requirement of successful ministry. No one calls themself; they are called by God. Their responsibility is to respond. Moses argued against His call, but God won the argument. Jonah tried to run away from God's call, but God won the race. God is still calling today. The harvest is ripe, but the laborers are few. Everyone who hears God's call must respond!

God has called some unlikely people for His projects. I shall name three here. First, when God had a big project to accomplish, He called a failed man named Moses. By circumstances only God could orchestrate, Moses, a Jewish boy, became a prince of Egypt. Through the foolishness of youth and an impetuous passion for justice, he made serious mistakes and lost everything. The miracle boy became a fugitive and fled to the Midianite country. There he married and decided to live an insignificant life of labor and servitude as a shepherd, serving his father-in-law, Jethro. Moses was minding his own business, settled in his minimum-wage job, glad to be alive after escaping the sword of the pharaoh for committing murder. By all measures, this laborer in the desert was finished!

But one day everything changed in his life! On a mountainside, he saw a bush on fire. Strangely, the fire was not consuming the bush. He was drawn to it and then shocked as he heard his name being called out from the burning bush. It was the voice of God.

> So when the LORD saw that he turned aside to look, God called to him from the midst of the bush and said, "Moses, Moses!"
>
> And he said, "Here I am."
>
> Then He said, "Do not draw near this place. Take your sandals off your feet, for the place where you stand is holy ground." Moreover, He said, "I am the God of your father—the God of Abraham, the God of Isaac, and the God of Jacob." And Moses hid his face, for he was afraid to look upon God. (Ex. 3:4–6)

The call of God had a tremendous impact on Moses. The vision of the bush on fire and the power of the voice gripped him. On that hillside his life moved from ordinary to extraordinary. The God he had heard about from his mother long ago appeared to him, and the encounter invaded his low estate. He was on familiar ground, but he stood a new way on it that day. The common ground he had treaded with the sheep he did not own became holy ground. Moses was in the presence of the holy and he was changed. His story changed there as he heard the voice of God clarify the purpose of the encounter.

> And the LORD said: "I have surely seen the oppression of My people who are in Egypt, and have heard their cry

> because of their taskmasters, for I know their sorrows. So I have come down to deliver them out of the hand of the Egyptians, and to bring them up from that land to a good and large land, to a land flowing with milk and honey, to the place of the Canaanites and the Hittites and the Amorites and the Perizzites and the Hivites and the Jebusites. Now therefore, behold, the cry of the children of Israel has come to Me, and I have also seen the oppression with which the Egyptians oppress them. Come now, therefore, and I will send you to Pharaoh that you may bring My people, the children of Israel, out of Egypt. (vv. 7–10)

Standing barefooted, Moses saw things differently for the first time. He was never the same again. He stopped looking for the answers to the puzzling questions of his life and decided to be part of the answer. His attention was withdrawn from the past and refocused on the future God had for him. He traded his story for God's bigger story on that day. His new future began there, on that mountainside.

Moses was not called until he had lost everything—family, home, community, and maybe the throne. The call came after forty years of wandering in the desert, and it came only after he became comfortable with his failed life. When he least expected it, he received the invitation to the adventure God had for him.

We know the rest of the story. Moses went as God commanded and he was instrumental in delivering his people from their oppressive Egyptian masters. His descendants are still there today to tell the story of their deliverance.

God's call is never too late. He calls not just the young and the successful; God calls whomever He wants. Blessed are those who respond to God's call in obedience.

The next witness is Elijah. He taught us that when God had a transgenerational project, He could call a depressed prophet. The story is in 1 Kings 18–19. Elijah was on Mount Carmel, confronting the prophets of Baal. He challenged them to bring down fire from heaven to burn a sacrificial offering. They failed. Elijah, however, prayed to Jehovah: "LORD God of Abraham, Isaac, and Israel, let it be known this day that You are God in Israel and I am Your servant, and that I have done all these things at Your word" (1 Kings 18:36). God answered all three requests: He revealed who God was, He revealed who Elijah was, and He revealed that His purpose was to turn the hearts of the people back to Him. Fire came down from heaven and burned up the offering! However, after being highly successful in turning the people's hearts back to God, Elijah found himself deeply discouraged due to the threat promised by the queen of the land, Jezebel. He thought that death might be preferable to this threatened situation.

While sleeping under a juniper tree in the wilderness:

> An angel touched him, and said to him, "Arise and eat." Then he looked, and there by his head was a cake baked on coals, and a jar of water. So he ate and drank, and lay down again. And the angel of the LORD came back the second time, and touched him, and said, "Arise and eat, because the journey is too great for you." So he arose, and ate and drank; and he went in

> the strength of that food forty days and forty nights as far as Horeb, the mountain of God. (1 Kings 19:5–8).

There Elijah encountered God again and received a commission:

> Go, return on your way to the Wilderness of Damascus; and when you arrive, anoint Hazael as king over Syria. Also you shall anoint Jehu the son of Nimshi as king over Israel. And Elisha the son of Shaphat of Abel Meholah you shall anoint as prophet in your place. (vv. 15–16)

Most noticeable here is the commission to ordain his replacement. Elijah must ordain Elisha to continue the prophetic ministry. Elijah obeyed God, and Elisha discovered God's purpose for his life—received his call—and began his journey of faith and in some ways his ministry exceeded that of his mentor.

The third example is an unlikely candidate for ministry. In this case God wanted to touch someone from a faraway place, someone of a different race and nationality, and He called a deacon named Philip to accomplish it. Philip received his call from the words of an angel. He was already commissioned by the apostles to serve at the table: "And they chose Stephen, a man full of faith and the Holy Spirit, and Philip, Prochorus, Nicanor, Timon, Parmenas, and Nicolas, a proselyte from Antioch, whom they set before the apostles; and when they had prayed, they laid hands on them" (Acts 6:5–6).

But Philip had a special intercontinental mission, and God through an angel commissioned him. "Now an angel of the

Lord spoke to Philip, saying, 'Arise and go toward the south along the road which goes down from Jerusalem to Gaza.' This is desert" (Acts 8:26).

Philip went to the desert and encountered a eunuch who was the Ethiopian minister of finance on his way back to his homeland. Philip preached to him, and the Ethiopian was converted and baptized in the desert. This eunuch became the first missionary to his own people. God wanted to touch a nation through a minister of state, and he called an unlikely person like Philip to accomplish it.

Ministry Today

God is concerned about the continuation of ministry. He is looking for those who will speak for Him to their respective generations. Ministry is leadership, and God calls people to give leadership to His people in each generation.

Often the appointment happens during transitions. Samuel was called when Eli the priest had lost his vision and his effectiveness as a leader. David became the leader of Israel when Saul lost his anointing. Elisha replaced Elijah when he was ready to retire. Isaiah heard God's call during a transition. He testified, "I heard the voice of the LORD, saying: 'Whom shall I send, and who will go for Us?' Then I said, 'Here am I! Send me" (Isa. 6:8).

Jesus called the twelve. Paul and Barnabas discerned God's call on their lives and the church recognized it publicly.

Christian ministry is a total response to God's call on a person's life (2 Tim. 1:9; 1 Thess. 2:12).[40] While the Bible acknowledges the priesthood of all believers, it clearly indicates that God calls certain individuals for specific tasks and offices of ministry. Scripture defines ministry as being a coworker with God, carrying out His purposes in the world (John 4:34; 2 Cor. 6:1). The almighty God chooses to depend on fragile human beings to complete His work of restoration, reconciliation, and redemption in this fallen world. Ministry is, therefore, doing God's will in the world. But before God's will can be carried out, it must be sought in prayer. Ministry, then, is seeking God's will in prayer and doing His will through one's life (1 John 2:17).

Ordained ministers are not expected to carry out all the work of the ministry. God gave apostles, prophets, evangelists, pastors, and teachers for the equipping of the believers to do the work of the ministry, according to Ephesians 4:12. To a large degree, ministry is simply equipping and enabling other believers to fulfill the multiple ministries of God's church. The ultimate purpose of ministry is, therefore, to produce people who minister. Although not all are called to the offices of ministry, all believers are called to minister. True ministry is enabling others to serve in the name of Jesus by edifying, equipping, and helping them to grow.

Christian ministry involves bringing people into a vital relationship with God through Jesus Christ (2 Cor. 5:20). It is also the proclamation (*kerygma*) of the gospel of Jesus Christ (2 Tim. 4:2, 5). As people are reconciled with God, they are also called to be reconciled with one another; therefore, one can say that biblical ministry is a relational enterprise involving the work of reconciliation.

Scripture confirms that ministry is the vocation of being involved in discipleship and spiritual formation. A minister is called to bring wholeness to individuals: "May your whole spirit, soul, and body be preserved blameless at the coming of our Lord Jesus Christ" (1 Thess. 5:23). According to this text, biblical wholeness is holiness. God calls His broken children to wholeness and holiness; therefore, ministry must seek to restore persons to wholeness and holiness through discipleship and spiritual formation. This also includes bringing healing to body, mind, spirit, and relationships.

True ministry can only be accomplished through a life of servanthood to God and others in the name of Christ (Gal. 5:13; 6:2, 5). *Diakonia* means service. The highest title in the kingdom of God is that of servant; thus, leadership in God's church must be servant leadership.

Scripture also emphasizes the importance of *koinonia*, the fellowship of believers and the communion of saints (1 John 1:7). Ministry involves facilitating this fellowship and communion in the body of Christ.

In essence, ministry is one's obedient response to God's call manifested as an advanced level of discipleship and the ongoing work of disciple making. Ministers are a gift of God to the church (Eph. 4:11), and they are representatives of God who plead with the world to be reconciled with God (2 Cor. 5:18–19). A minister, as an ambassador, must dialogue with the world while at the same time remaining in constant communication with God. The pastoral epistles list other ministerial duties, including reproving, rebuking, exhorting, enduring, and doing the work of an evangelist (2 Tim. 4:2–5). They also include equipping, perfecting, edifying, unifying, and bringing persons to maturity (Eph. 4:12). This is the work of disciple making and spiritual formation.

Parents, teachers, and pastors do not call people to ministry, although all of them can influence people in positive ways in this regard. In fact, no one should venture out to enter vocational ministry just because their mother or father told them to do so, even when a parent happens to be a minister. Bible colleges and seminaries cannot call people to ministry either; they can only train people for Christian service. It is God who calls. The first step to becoming a Spirit-empowered minister is to discern one's call. God's call is not always dramatic or necessarily at a specific time and place. In some cases, it may be similar to the dramatic calls of Moses, Isaiah, and Paul, but in most situations it is much less sensational. In many cases it may be an unremarkable process involving very ordinary people and some divine appointments. Many people find themselves on their way to prepare for some other profession or being involved in some other business when they discern God's call.

It appears that God calls people for His service who are busy with something else entrusted to them. For instance, Moses was busy tending Jethro's sheep when God called him (Ex. 3:1). Gideon was busy threshing wheat (Judg. 6:11). David was in the field with sheep and fighting wild animals to protect them (1 Sam. 16:1–11). Elisha was plowing with twelve yokes of oxen (1 Kings 19:19). Amos was busy leading sheep (Amos 1:1). Peter and Andrew were busy fishing when Jesus called them to follow Him (Matt. 4:18–20). James and John were mending their nets (Matt. 4:21). Matthew was collecting taxes (Matt. 9:9), and Saul of Tarsus was busy persecuting the followers of Jesus (Acts 9:1–2).

I was studying physics with the hope of becoming a scientist when I sensed God's call. Having watched different people respond differently to God's call to full-time Christian service from the perspective of a theological educator and ministry trainer, my suggestion to young disciples feeling a sense of call to vocational ministry is to yield to the call of God as early as possible. I know individuals who disobeyed or postponed what they sensed as God's call due to family, fear, or ambitions, and then they were miserable later in life. I have also watched some who eventually returned to their original calling but made themselves and others miserable by trying to overcompensate for lost time. It is better to be like young Samuel and say, "Speak, for Your servant hears" (1 Sam. 3:10).

Remember that God's call normally follows a process, as Richard Niebuhr suggested. Pay attention to this process and don't be afraid to check with your "disciplers" to validate your perceptions. You don't need to bargain with God as if He is calling you to some kind of misery. Discover God's will as you would in any other situation and simply make yourself available to Him. Don't be drawn by perceived status or other attractions of ministry. There is nothing wrong with having a desire to be a minister because, according to Paul, a person desiring to be a minister is seeking a good thing (1 Tim. 3:1); make sure you are motivated by a desire to serve God and His people.

It is very unusual for anyone to know God's ultimate plans for their life at the beginning of this process. In most cases, we must step out in faith at some point, based on the light we have received, because discovering God's ultimate purpose can be a lifelong process. Recall that Paul first said that God called him on his way to Damascus (Acts 26:16). Later he said that God called him while he was in his mother's womb (Gal. 1:15). Further down the road in his journey of faith, Paul said God's call took place "before time began" (2 Tim. 1:9)! We can only conclude that the longer we serve God, the deeper we understand His plans and purposes for us.

Don't be afraid to step out in faith based on what you already know. I guarantee this will be an exciting journey of discovery. I have never regretted not becoming a scientist. It is hard to prove, but even my study of physics and mathematics has helped me in fulfilling God's assignment to serve as a seminary dean.

Matching Training with Calling

Let me share a word about the matter of preparation for vocational ministry. Here is the rule of thumb: your preparation must match your calling. Once you discern your calling, you should seek counsel regarding the training required to fulfill that call adequately. Some may need only institute-level training to fulfill their calling. Others may require graduation from a Bible college or seminary. Others, like those called to seminary teaching, need doctoral-level training. I do not look down on any level of ministerial training. I believe all levels of training are needed. Your training should prepare you for your calling.

This means some readers will have to go to school and stay there for a lengthy period of time while others need to quit expensive higher education in theology and seek a more appropriate level of training. I compare the longer stay in school to the time a plane spends on the runway. Normally, larger planes needing to stay in the air longer spend more time on the runway as they take off. Smaller planes can take off faster from shorter runways, but they don't stay as long in the air or fly as high as the bigger ones. This is why discovering one's calling is such a vital step. I have seen some people stay too long in school, others leave too soon, and yet another group refuses to enter a training process. Peter and Paul did not have the same academic preparation or capacity, but both were effective in their ministries. What is God calling you to do? Prepare for it.

Keep in mind you don't have to be fully prepared for lifelong service at the beginning of your ministry, as there are differing assignments within the same general calling. You will have opportunities to prepare more fully for special assignments as you go forward. For instance, you may begin your work as a pastor and then sense a leading to a specialized ministry, such as chaplaincy or seminary teaching. I did not begin ministry expecting to be a chaplain, seminary professor, or dean. I felt a call to be a pastor, and eventually, within that call, I found the other assignments. As a dean, I saw myself as a pastor to the faculty and staff and the students at large, although my daily duties included seminary leadership and higher education administration. I became a lifelong learner and received the education and training I needed as various doors opened. God used several people (who could be called disciple makers) to speak into my life at crucial moments in my journey. They encouraged me, mentored me, and stood by me when I needed them. They also provided a sense of accountability. Make sure you keep some Barnabases in your life.

Ministry and Discipleship

The Gospels are full of images of ministry and discipleship. David W. Bennett, in *Metaphors of Ministry*, categorizes these as images of people and images of things.[41] Some images are relationship oriented while others are task oriented. Relationship-oriented images include those of brother, sister, child, son, friend, guest, and disciple. According to Bennett, images of servant, manager, shepherd, worker, apostle, witness, and fisherman are primarily task-oriented metaphors. Scripture uses commonplace things such as soil, field, firstfruits, vines and branches, wheat, sheep, salt, light, building, and body to bear the image of ministry.

From these images Bennett draws certain metaphoric themes. First, he sees the theme of weakness and dependence in biblical ministry. Ministers are weak vessels on their own, but they can depend on God for strength. Bennett sees a second theme of honor and dignity in biblical ministry. It is an honor to be a minister of the gospel; God calls His children to be vessels of honor, and they bring glory to God when they serve honorably. Bennett also sees the theme of interconnection in biblical ministry in images such as branch, building, and body. Ministry involves connecting people to God and connecting people to people. Ministers connect people in a disconnected world, which makes ministry a vocation of inclusion rather than exclusion.

Ministers fulfill many roles. Functionally, they participate in the community and engage in doing the many life-giving tasks needed within the community. Regardless of their position, ministers are people who serve under authority; ministers also have authority, but they are not to become authoritarian. Ultimately, ministers are called to identify with Jesus in the pattern of His life, and ministers are accountable to Christ for their character and service.

Christian ministry is the continuing legacy of the ministry of Jesus of Nazareth. Jesus was an apostle of God, and He came to proclaim and inaugurate the kingdom of God. An apostle is one who is sent. The Father sent Jesus, and Jesus sent twelve envoys. We are to receive Him and those whom He sent: "Let us go. . . . That is why I have come" (Mark 1:38 NIV). Scripture tells us that those who received the disciples also received Jesus: "He who receives you receives Me" (Matt. 10:40). Ministry is the work of those who are sent by Jesus.

Jesus was the ideal servant, fulfilling the biblical prophecies of the suffering servant. The disciples were to follow His example of servanthood (John 13:5); they were not to "lord it over" others (Matt. 20:25–28). Among His disciples, the greatest was to become the servant of all (Matt. 23:11).

Jesus' ministry was powerful because of the presence and power of the Holy Spirit in His life. Jesus was conceived by the Spirit (Matt. 1:20, 23). The Holy Spirit came upon Him at the time of His baptism (Mark 1:8–11), and the Spirit drove Him to the wilderness to be tempted (Luke 4:1). He returned from the wilderness in the power of the Holy Spirit (Luke 4:14) to carry out His ministry (Mark 13:11; Matt. 10:20; Luke 12:12; John 14:15–17; 15:26). Jesus promised the outpouring of the Holy Spirit on His disciples (Luke 24:49); their ministry was to be characterized by the empowerment of the Holy Spirit. The Spirit was to enable them to speak (Mark 13:11), to testify, and to bear witness. Jesus—the apostle, the servant, and the one who was led by the Spirit—was the ministry role model for His disciples, and He remains the same for all who will follow their example.

Mark the evangelist presented the essence of ministry as he outlined Jesus' ministry: "Then He appointed twelve, that they might be with Him and that He might send them out to preach, and to have power to heal sicknesses and to cast out demons" (Mark 3:14–15). Performance of ministry tasks was of secondary importance to the primary call of the disciple *to be with Jesus.* The disciples were called to preach and to drive out demons, but being with Jesus was their priority. They were set apart to be with Him first, and then to set the captives free.

Unfortunately, not everyone follows God's call. For instance, Saul went searching for his father's donkeys even as God was calling him to be a king. He was unaware of God's presence in his life and God's plan for his future. Samuel had to stop Saul in his tracks to bring the message of God's call to his attention (1 Sam. 9:27–10:1). Jonah ran from his call to preach to Nineveh and ran away to Tarshish, only to encounter a tempest that led him to repentance and to return to his assignment (Jonah 3:1–3). Paul wrote about Demas, who forsook his call and went back into the world (2 Tim. 4:10). Demas had great potential, but it was never realized.

Let me conclude this section by simply advising every reader to follow God's call, regardless of where it might lead. Based on scores of testimonies and my own experience, I can promise that you will not regret that decision. Remember there are many ways to impact the world for God.

CHAPTER 7

DISCIPLESHIP, MINISTRY, AND SUFFERING

So [Peter and the other apostles] departed from the presence of the council, rejoicing that they were counted worthy to suffer shame for His name. (Acts 5:41)

For I consider that the sufferings of this present time are not worthy to be compared with the glory which shall be revealed in us. (Rom. 8:18)

It is hard for some to believe that suffering is a part of discipleship and ministry. The Bible is very clear about the cost of discipleship: "Then He said to them all, 'If anyone desires to come after Me, let him deny himself, and take up his cross daily, and follow Me'" (Luke 9:23). It appears the cost of discipleship is threefold:

1. Deny ourselves, which means giving up the pleasures of sin.

2. Take up our cross, which means finding our place of service in the name of Jesus.
3. And follow the Lord, which means identifying with Jesus fully and following in His footsteps.

The first requirement—deny ourselves—is giving up the pleasures of sin and avoiding worldly corruption. Paul said, "Nevertheless the solid foundation of God stands, having this seal: 'The Lord knows those who are His,' and, 'Let everyone who names the name of Christ depart from iniquity'" (2 Tim. 2:19). Peter recommended the same to his readers: "Beloved, I beg you as sojourners and pilgrims, abstain from fleshly lusts which war against the soul" (1 Pet. 2:11). Paul urged his young disciple Timothy: "But you, O man of God, flee these things and pursue righteousness, godliness, faith, love, patience, gentleness. Fight the good fight of faith, lay hold on eternal life, to which you were also called and have confessed the good confession in the presence of many witnesses" (1 Tim. 6:11–12). He gave this example in his second letter to Timothy: "No one engaged in warfare entangles himself with the affairs of this life, that he may please him who enlisted him as a soldier" (2 Tim. 2:4).

Denying oneself will also mean avoiding even permissible things under certain circumstances. For instance, Paul told the Corinthians, "All things are lawful for me, but not all things are helpful; all things are lawful for me, but not all things edify. Let no one seek his own, but each one the other's well-being" (1 Cor. 10:23–24). He gave a practical example of this to the Roman believers: "Do not destroy the work of God for the sake of food. All things indeed are pure, but it is evil for the man who eats with offense. It is good neither to eat meat nor drink wine nor do anything by which your brother stumbles or is offended or is made weak" (Rom. 14:20–21).

Taking up the cross also conveys the idea of willingly offering sacrificial service in the name of Christ. Inconveniences, persecutions, thanklessness, etc., should be incurred in the service of God. These are not acceptable excuses to stop following Jesus. "No one, having put his hand to the plow, and looking back, is fit for the kingdom of God" (Luke 9:62).

Following Jesus involves going where He leads, even to tough places, and this must be done without delay. The time to follow is now. Paul explained, "For [the Lord] says: 'In an acceptable time I have heard you, and in the day of salvation I have helped you.' Behold, now is the accepted time; behold, now is the day of salvation" (2 Cor. 6:2). We must not only go where He leads, we must also do whatever He says. This is what Peter was practicing in Jerusalem: "So they called them and commanded them not to speak at all nor teach in the name of Jesus. But Peter and John answered and said to them, 'Whether it is right in the sight of God to listen to you more than to God, you judge. For we cannot but speak the things which we have seen and heard'" (Acts 4:18–20). This is not a short-term appointment. This is a lifelong commitment. A disciple must follow Jesus on this costly journey forever. This is an everlasting relationship. Jesus said: "My sheep hear My voice, and I know them, and they follow Me. And I give them eternal life, and they shall never perish; neither shall anyone snatch them out of My hand" (John 10:27–28).

There is no true discipleship without a cost. Authentic Christian living encounters suffering and pain. Suffering can deconstruct the fake versions of life we prefer to live and can enhance our faith and our relationship with Jesus Christ. Suffering strengthens the believer. As disciples of Jesus, we are not to seek pain and suffering but must be willing to encounter them as part of following Christ and becoming more like Him. Loving our neighbor as ourselves is a concept related to Christian mission. As we are engaged in sharing our faith with others, our hearts are reshaped, and our minds are transformed. This often involves encountering pain and suffering.

All disciples should understand that persecution and suffering are part of authentic Christian living. The suffering of the innocent does not make sense, but it is not a hidden fact of discipleship. Paul made it very clear to Timothy: "Yes, and all who desire to live godly in Christ Jesus will suffer persecution" (2 Tim. 3:12). The Bible makes the following truths about discipleship very plain. First, all followers of Jesus will encounter trials and tribulations: "In this you greatly rejoice, though now for a little while, if need be, you have been grieved by various trials, that the genuineness of your faith, being much more precious than gold that perishes, though it is tested by fire, may be found to praise, honor, and glory at the revelation of Jesus Christ" (1 Pet. 1:6–7).

Second, we can cause our own suffering through personal sinfulness. All disciples should live self-examined lives, because not all suffering is caused by Satan or the world. Recognize that sometimes God is chastening His beloved for their own benefit. Hear Paul's admonition: "But let a man examine himself, and so let him eat of the bread and drink of the cup. For he who eats and drinks in an unworthy manner eats and drinks judgment to himself, not discerning the Lord's body. For this reason many are weak and sick among you, and many sleep. For if we would judge ourselves, we would not be judged. But when we are judged, we are chastened by the Lord, that we may not be condemned with the world" (1 Cor. 11:28–32). The writer of Hebrews explained why a disciple should endure God's chastening:

> If you endure chastening, God deals with you as with sons; for what son is there whom a father does not chasten? But if you are without chastening, of which all have become partakers, then you are illegitimate and not sons. Furthermore, we have had human fathers who corrected us, and we paid them respect. Shall we not much more readily be in subjection to the Father of spirits and live? For they indeed for a few days chastened us as seemed best to them, but He for our profit, that we may be partakers of His holiness. Now no chastening seems to be joyful for the present, but painful; nevertheless, afterward it yields the peaceable fruit of righteousness to those who have been trained by it. (Heb. 12:7–11)

Third, it is better to suffer for doing good in the name of Jesus rather than for doing evil: "For it is better, if it is the will of God, to suffer for doing good than for doing evil" (1 Pet. 3:17). Finally, we must remember that if God chastens us, it is for our own benefit and the experience should be seen as an expression of His love, not hate. Paul testified of receiving God's chastening to prevent him from being exalted above measure by his calling and giftedness:

And lest I should be exalted above measure by the abundance of the revelations, a thorn in the flesh was given to me, a messenger of Satan to buffet me, lest I be exalted above measure. Concerning this thing I pleaded with the Lord three times that it might depart from me. And He said to me, "My grace is sufficient for you, for My strength is made perfect in weakness." Therefore most gladly I will rather boast in my infirmities, that the power of Christ may rest upon me. Therefore I take pleasure in infirmities, in reproaches, in needs, in persecutions, in distresses, for Christ's sake. For when I am weak, then I am strong. (2 Cor. 12:7–10)

Dealing with Suffering

How does one cope with suffering? Certainly, one should believe that God will not test His children beyond their ability to endure. God will provide His grace to cope with any given situation. He will also make a way of escape. God has promised His presence regardless of the situation we face or its duration. The following are some things to remember when one goes through suffering.

1. Remember that Jesus is our example in suffering. We can look to Him.

> For to this you were called, because Christ also suffered for us, leaving us an example, that you should follow His steps. (1 Pet. 2:21)

2. Remember that all things work together for good.

> And we know that all things work together for good to those who love God, to those who are the called according to His purpose. (Rom. 8:28)

3. Remember to examine oneself without blaming oneself or others.

Now as Jesus passed by, He saw a man who was blind from birth. And His disciples asked Him, saying, "Rabbi, who sinned, this man or his parents, that he was born blind?"

Jesus answered, "Neither this man nor his parents sinned, but that the works of God should be revealed in him." (John 9:1–3)

For whom the LORD loves He chastens,
And scourges every son whom He receives. (Heb. 12:6)

4. Remember that God may have purposes for our suffering beyond our current understanding.

And you became followers of us and of the Lord, having received the word in much affliction, with joy of the Holy Spirit, so that you became examples to all in Macedonia and Achaia who believe. (1 Thess. 1:6–7)

5. Remember that a disciple's ultimate purpose is to be conformed to the image of God's Son, Jesus.

That I may know Him and the power of His resurrection, and the fellowship of His sufferings, being conformed to His death, if, by any means, I may attain to the resurrection from the dead. (Phil. 3:10–11)

6. Remember that all our suffering is only for a moment with respect to eternity.

> For I consider that the sufferings of this present time are not worthy to be compared with the glory which shall be revealed in us. (Rom 8:18)

Wisdom from Paul

Paul the apostle established a clear connection between vocational ministry and suffering. He described his ministry in Ephesus in his farewell address in Acts 20. One can discern five characteristics of his ministry there.

1. Paul's ministry was tearful.

> Serving the Lord with all humility, with many tears and trials which happened to me by the plotting of the Jews. (v. 19)
>
> Therefore watch, and remember that for three years I did not cease to warn everyone night and day with tears. (v. 31)
>
> And when he had said these things, he knelt down and prayed with them all. Then they all wept freely, and fell on Paul's neck and kissed him, sorrowing most of all for the words which he spoke, that they would see his face no more. And they accompanied him to the ship. (vv. 36–38)

2. Paul's ministry was faithful.

> I kept back nothing that was helpful, but proclaimed it to you, and taught you publicly and from house to house, testifying to Jews, and also to Greeks, repentance toward God and faith toward our Lord Jesus Christ. And see, now I go bound in the spirit to Jerusalem,

not knowing the things that will happen to me there, except that the Holy Spirit testifies in every city, saying that chains and tribulations await me. But none of these things move me; nor do I count my life dear to myself, so that I may finish my race with joy, and the ministry which I received from the Lord Jesus, to testify to the gospel of the grace of God.

And indeed, now I know that you all, among whom I have gone preaching the kingdom of God, will see my face no more. Therefore I testify to you this day that I am innocent of the blood of all men. For I have not shunned to declare to you the whole counsel of God. (vv. 20–27)

3. Paul's ministry was self-examining, watchful, and pastoral.

Therefore take heed to yourselves and to all the flock, among which the Holy Spirit has made you overseers, to shepherd the church of God which He purchased with His own blood. For I know this, that after my departure savage wolves will come in among you, not sparing the flock. Also from among yourselves men will rise up, speaking perverse things, to draw away the disciples after themselves. Therefore watch, and remember that for three years I did not cease to warn everyone night and day with tears. (vv. 28–31)

4. Paul's ministry was eschatological.

So now, brethren, I commend you to God and to the word of His grace, which is able to build you up

> and give you an inheritance among all those who are sanctified. (v. 32)
>
> 5. Paul's ministry was sacrificial.
>
> I have coveted no one's silver or gold or apparel. Yes, you yourselves know that these hands have provided for my necessities, and for those who were with me. I have shown you in every way, by laboring like this, that you must support the weak. And remember the words of the Lord Jesus, that He said, "It is more blessed to give than to receive." (vv. 33–35)

The apostle's letters to the first-century churches provide a catalogue of the suffering he endured to fulfill God's call on his life as a disciple maker, servant of God, and apostle. I am not suggesting that every minister should suffer in these ways; however, disciples who wish to grow in the grace and knowledge of the Lord Jesus Christ and who desire to be involved in the life-giving vocation of ministry should have no illusion about the cost of authentic discipleship and ministry. Let us review some of what Paul endured.

1. Paul had physical infirmities.

The apostle said, "You know that because of physical infirmity I preached the gospel to you at the first" (Gal. 4:13). Others testified to his weakness in body: "'For his letters,' they say, 'are weighty and powerful, but his bodily presence is weak, and his speech contemptible'" (2 Cor. 10:10). Paul suffered from visual deficiencies: "See with what large letters I have written to you with my own hand" (Gal. 6:11). He suffered from what he described as a thorn in the flesh:

And lest I should be exalted above measure by the abundance of the revelations, a thorn in the flesh was given to me, a messenger of Satan to buffet me, lest I be exalted above measure. Concerning this thing I pleaded with the Lord three times that it might depart from me. And He said to me, "My grace is sufficient for you, for My strength is made perfect in weakness." Therefore most gladly I will rather boast in my infirmities, that the power of Christ may rest upon me. Therefore I take pleasure in infirmities, in reproaches, in needs, in persecutions, in distresses, for Christ's sake. For when I am weak, then I am strong. (2 Cor. 12:7–10)

2. Paul experienced weariness, sleeplessness, and great concern for the churches.

Are they Hebrews? So am I. Are they Israelites? So am I. Are they the seed of Abraham? So am I. Are they ministers of Christ?—I speak as a fool—I am more: in labors more abundant, in stripes above measure, in prisons more frequently, in deaths often. From the Jews five times I received forty stripes minus one. Three times I was beaten with rods; once I was stoned; three times I was shipwrecked; a night and a day I have been in the deep; in journeys often, in perils of waters, in perils of robbers, in perils of my own countrymen, in perils of the Gentiles, in perils in the city, in perils in the wilderness, in perils in the sea, in perils among false brethren; in weariness and toil, in sleeplessness often, in hunger and thirst, in fastings often, in cold

> and nakedness—besides the other things, what comes upon me daily: my deep concern for all the churches. (2 Cor. 11:22–28)

3. Paul had undefined suffering in his ministry.

> I now rejoice in my sufferings for you, and fill up in my flesh what is lacking in the afflictions of Christ, for the sake of His body, which is the church, of which I became a minister according to the stewardship from God which was given to me for you, to fulfill the word of God. (Col. 1:24–25)

4. Paul experienced afflictions.

> But you have carefully followed my doctrine, manner of life, purpose, faith, longsuffering, love, perseverance, persecutions, afflictions, which happened to me at Antioch, at Iconium, at Lystra—what persecutions I endured. And out of them all the Lord delivered me. (2 Tim. 3:10–11)

5. Paul carried burdens beyond his strength, even to the point of despair.

> For we do not want you to be ignorant, brethren, of our trouble which came to us in Asia: that we were burdened beyond measure, above strength, so that we despaired even of life. (2 Cor. 1:8)

He was confronted with his mortality at crucial times: "Yes, we had the sentence of death in ourselves, that we should not trust in ourselves but in God who raises the dead" (2 Cor. 1:9).

6. Paul was beaten and wounded.

Paul was whipped and locked up in Philippi: "And when they had laid many stripes on them, they threw them into prison, commanding the jailer to keep them securely. Having received such a charge, he put them into the inner prison and fastened their feet in the stocks" (Acts 16:23–24). Paul told the Galatians, "From now on let no one trouble me, for I bear in my body the marks of the Lord Jesus" (Gal. 6:17).

Of course, Paul was delivered from distress on many occasions. He experienced divine interventions in profound ways. He overcame pain and suffering by the grace of God and by dependence on the Holy Spirit. Deep faith in God and His faithfulness sustained Paul. He believed that "all things work together for good to those who love God, to those who are the called according to His purpose" (Rom. 8:28). He knew that nothing would separate him from God's love. Listen to his declaration:

> Who shall separate us from the love of Christ? Shall trouble or hardship or persecution or famine or nakedness or danger or sword? As it is written:
>
> "For your sake we face death all day long;
> we are considered as sheep to be slaughtered."
>
> No, in all these things we are more than conquerors through him who loved us. For I am convinced that neither death nor life, neither angels nor demons, neither the present nor the future, nor any powers, neither height nor depth, nor anything else in all creation, will be able to separate us from the love of God that is in Christ Jesus our Lord. (Rom. 8:35–39 NIV)

Paul was not only able to overcome his suffering but also able to glory in his tribulations because he had an unshakable eschatological perspective: "For I consider that the sufferings of this present time are not worthy to be compared with the glory which shall be revealed in us" (Rom. 8:18).

It is only natural for disciples to wonder why they are suffering without cause. Jesus addressed this issue with His disciples on the occasion of the healing of a blind man. Recall John's report:

> As he went along, he saw a man blind from birth. His disciples asked him, "Rabbi, who sinned, this man or his parents, that he was born blind?"
>
> "Neither this man nor his parents sinned," said Jesus, "but this happened so that the works of God might be displayed in him." (John 9:1–3 NIV)

The Bible gives the best understanding of suffering, but it does not give a full explanation of all suffering. Jesus did not explain suffering, but He did everything He could to alleviate suffering and trained His disciples to do the same.

Not Explaining the Unexplainable

We should not try to ascertain the exact cause of each incident of suffering. It is better to wait for better understanding or to leave these things to God. We know that suffering can result from personal and corporate sin and by the sinful nature of this fallen world. The German theologian Dietrich Bonhoeffer said that we live "between the curse and the promise."[42] Sometimes the best answer to questions regarding the cause of profound suffering is "I don't know." It is better not to explain the unexplainable. George Buttrick said that to cope with suffering, "What we need is not an explanation, but a salvation."[43]

In *Christ and Human Suffering*,[44] E. Stanley Jones said that suffering comes to us through nine avenues:

1. From confused counsels in religion
2. From ways and conflicts in human society
3. From physical calamities in nature
4. From physical sickness and infirmities
5. From economic distress
6. From acts of our colleagues
7. From religious and secular authorities
8. Through our home life and possibly an unhappy marriage
9. From being associated with Christ

Jones pointed out that the suffering of Christ is the central theme of the gospel and the cross is at the center of Christian faith. God in Jesus suffered on the cross. He participated in human suffering at the cross, making the darkest hour of history the brightest. So suffering makes sense in only one way: in the light of the cross and the resurrection of Jesus. Jones said that through the suffering of Jesus, God turned the darkest moment in history into the brightest. During times of great suffering, it is better to let all of God's people see this bright spot.

C. S. Lewis would agree. In his book *The Problem of Pain*, Lewis balanced Christian hope and a call to repentance: "God whispers to us in our pleasures, speaks in our conscience, and shouts in our pains."[45] While going through pain, loss, and suffering, especially for the cause of Christ, we must trust our Savior and hope in our loving God.

The apostle James gave the best advice: "Is anyone among you suffering? Let him pray. Is anyone cheerful? Let him sing psalms" (James 5:13). Peter gave a very similar exhortation: "But rejoice to the extent that you partake of Christ's sufferings, that when His glory is revealed, you may also be glad with exceeding joy" (1 Pet. 4:13).

I conclude this section with the following reminders for disciples who are at different stages of development.

1. Remember, you are not alone in your suffering.

> Be sober, be vigilant; because your adversary the devil walks about like a roaring lion, seeking whom he may devour. Resist him, steadfast in the faith, knowing that the same sufferings are experienced by your brotherhood in the world. (1 Pet. 5:8–9)

2. Suffering for Christ is pleasing to God.

> For this is commendable, if because of conscience toward God one endures grief, suffering wrongfully. (1 Pet. 2:19)
>
> Therefore do not be ashamed of the testimony of our Lord, nor of me His prisoner, but share with me in the sufferings for the gospel according to the power of God. (2 Tim. 1:8)

3. Ministry has suffering in it, but it is possible to rejoice in the suffering.

I now rejoice in my sufferings for you, and fill up in my flesh what is lacking in the afflictions of Christ, for the sake of His body, which is the church. (Col. 1:24)

4. Suffering is part of the transformational journey of faith.

That I may know Him and the power of His resurrection, and the fellowship of His sufferings, being conformed to His death. (Phil. 3:10)

5. The Lord will comfort His own who suffer.

For as the sufferings of Christ abound in us, so our consolation also abounds through Christ. (2 Cor. 1:5)

6. Suffering is not worthy to be compared with the glory that will be revealed in us.

For I consider that the sufferings of this present time are not worthy to be compared with the glory which shall be revealed in us. (Rom 8:18)

7. So pray, rejoice, and keep following Jesus.

Is anyone among you suffering? Let him pray. Is anyone cheerful? Let him sing psalms. (James 5:13)

But rejoice to the extent that you partake of Christ's sufferings, that when His glory is revealed, you may also be glad with exceeding joy. (1 Pet. 4:13)

To Be Like Jesus

Ultimately, a disciple is called to be like Jesus. So a disciple-making minister is called to be more like Jesus than others, because the minister is not only a disciple but also a coach in Christlikeness. What does it mean to be like Jesus? What does being like Jesus look like?

There are many ways to answer this question. Here is a practical way according to the Bible. First, one must love and forgive as Jesus did. He advised His disciples: "A new commandment I give to you, that you love one another; as I have loved you, that you also love one another. By this all will know that you are My disciples, if you have love for one another" (John 13:34–35). Paul's prayer for the Ephesians was they should be rooted and grounded in love: "That Christ may dwell in your hearts through faith; that you, being rooted and grounded in love, may be able to comprehend with all the saints what is the width and length and depth and height—to know the love of Christ which passes knowledge; that you may be filled with all the fullness of God" (Eph. 3:17–19). Jesus came to demonstrate the Father's love to help us to love as He did. He also modeled true forgiveness as He prayed for His enemies: "Father, forgive them, for they do not know what they do" (Luke 23:34). When we love and forgive, we are being like Jesus.

Such love leads to unity among His followers, not division. Jesus prayed:

> I do not pray for these alone, but also for those who will believe in Me through their word; that they all may be one, as You, Father, are in Me, and I in You; that they also may be one in Us, that the world may believe that You sent Me. And the glory which You

> gave Me I have given them, that they may be one just as We are one: I in them, and You in Me; that they may be made perfect in one, and that the world may know that You have sent Me, and have loved them as You have loved Me. (John 17:20–23)

True love also serves others instead of lording over them. To be like Jesus means we must serve one another in the name of Christ. Jesus demonstrated true service and servant leadership by washing His disciples' feet. John reported the Lord's words: "If I then, your Lord and Teacher, have washed your feet, you also ought to wash one another's feet. For I have given you an example, that you should do as I have done to you. Most assuredly, I say to you, a servant is not greater than his master; nor is he who is sent greater than he who sent him" (John 13:14–16).

Second, being like Jesus must mean living a sanctified life by the grace of God and by the help of the Holy Spirit. That is, we must make every effort to live in the world as if we do not belong to it: "They are not of the world, just as I am not of the world. Sanctify them by Your truth. Your word is truth. As You sent Me into the world, I also have sent them into the world. And for their sakes I sanctify Myself, that they also may be sanctified by the truth" (John 17:16–19). Biblically speaking, holiness means being set apart for God's use. Christians are called a holy brethren, a holy priesthood, and a holy temple: "Therefore, holy brethren, partakers of the heavenly calling, consider the Apostle and High Priest of our confession, Christ Jesus" (Heb. 3:1). Peter said: "You also, as living stones, are being built up a spiritual house, a holy priesthood, to offer up spiritual sacrifices acceptable to God through Jesus Christ" (1 Pet. 2:5). And Paul observed: "Do you not know that you are the temple of God and that the Spirit of God dwells in you? If anyone defiles the temple of God, God will destroy him. For the temple of God is holy, which temple you are" (1 Cor. 3:16–17). We must be actively involved in the pursuit of holiness.

There is a growing movement now that considers any effort by a believer to live a sanctified life as an unnecessary work of legalism. The chief proponent is the television preacher and personality Joseph Prince of Singapore. The following are major theological themes of what is referred to as hypergrace teaching:

1. Nothing you do will negatively affect your relationship with God.
2. As a believer, you never need to confess your sins to God or repent of your sins.
3. God doesn't see your sins because He always sees you as perfect through the blood of Jesus.
4. You can follow Jesus effortlessly.

Prince and his followers believe the doctrine of progressive sanctification is a "spiritually murderous lie" because the believer's future sins have already been forgiven. The teachings of Jesus before the cross do not apply to today's Christians, they teach.[46]

According to the doctrine of hypergrace, self-examination as it leads to sin consciousness should be discouraged to prevent believers from taking their eyes away from the finished work of Christ. As sins past, present, and future are already forgiven,

Christians do not have to repent. The Holy Spirit does not convict believers; He only convinces them of their righteousness. They consider the teachings on living a sanctified life as telling believers they are "saved by grace but perfected by human effort," producing "a Church that is judgmental, angry, hopeless, helpless, dependent, fearful, uninspired, ineffective, and perpetually spiritually immature." They consider Martin Luther's concept of grace and faith "utterly primitive." It is a profound mistake to assume the solution to having ineffective Christians in dead churches is hypergrace theology!

Prince's hypergrace doctrine is truly unbiblical. Versions of this false teaching have historically been referred to as antinomianism (i.e., I can live any way I wish) and have manifested since the early days of the church. The opposite of antinomianism is legalism. Sanctification is neither. The apostle Paul was very clear when he admonished the Corinthians regarding the Lord's table: "Therefore whoever eats this bread or drinks this cup of the Lord in an unworthy manner will be guilty of the body and blood of the Lord. But let a man examine himself, and so let him eat of the bread and drink of the cup" (1 Cor. 11:27–28). Scripture tells us that we must, in dependence upon the Holy Spirit, "strive" and "walk in step with the Spirit" with "diligence" and "perseverance."

Unfortunately, hypergrace theology confuses justification with sanctification, and it replaces progressive sanctification with realized sanctification. It seems to define all New Testament references to the law as meaning the Mosaic Law and relies on each believer to live a sanctified life by one's own strength, without the active participation with the Holy Spirit in the journey of faith called discipleship. Be cautious not to fall into this attractive trap!

Third, being like Jesus involves doing the works He did. Jesus promised that, through the power of the Spirit, His followers' work would exceed His own: "Most assuredly, I say to you, he who believes in Me, the works that I do he will do also; and greater works than these he will do, because I go to My Father" (John 14:12).

Holiness and Separation

Finally, being like Jesus demands the followers of Jesus live their lives in a way clearly distinguishable from the world. This is in line with the biblical history of the separation of God's people from the world. There was separation in Noah's time. God asked him to separate himself from his neighbors: "The end of all flesh has come before Me, for the earth is filled with violence through them; and behold, I will destroy them with the earth. Make yourself an ark of gopherwood; make rooms in the ark, and cover it inside and outside with pitch" (Gen. 6:13–14). There was separation during Lot's time also:

> Then the men said to Lot, "Have you anyone else here? Son-in-law, your sons, your daughters, and whomever you have in the city—take them out of this place! For we will destroy this place, because the outcry against them has grown great before the face of the LORD, and the LORD has sent us to destroy it."
>
> So Lot went out and spoke to his sons-in-law, who had married his daughters, and said, "Get up,

> get out of this place; for the LORD will destroy this city!" But to his sons-in-law he seemed to be joking. (Gen. 19:12–14)

The story of the Israelites was also a story of separation from their ungodly oppressors. God spoke to Moses:

> For I will pass through the land of Egypt on that night, and will strike all the firstborn in the land of Egypt, both man and beast; and against all the gods of Egypt I will execute judgment: I am the LORD. Now the blood shall be a sign for you on the houses where you are. And when I see the blood, I will pass over you; and the plague shall not be on you to destroy you when I strike the land of Egypt. (Ex. 12:12–13)

The separation of disciples from the kingdom of darkness should manifest in all areas of their life, including marriage and social life. Paul said:

> Do not be unequally yoked together with unbelievers. For what fellowship has righteousness with lawlessness? And what communion has light with darkness? And what accord has Christ with Belial? Or what part has a believer with an unbeliever? And what agreement has the temple of God with idols? For you are the temple of the living God. As God has said:
>
> "I will dwell in them
> And walk among them.
> I will be their God,
> And they shall be My people."

Therefore
"Come out from among them
And be separate, says the Lord.
Do not touch what is unclean,
And I will receive you." (2 Cor. 6:14–17)

The Bible anticipates a future separation between the righteous and the unrighteous. The parables of Jesus regarding the kingdom of God make this very clear. In the parable of the wheat and the tares, Jesus says, "Let both grow together until the harvest, and at the time of harvest I will say to the reapers, 'First gather together the tares and bind them in bundles to burn them, but gather the wheat into my barn'" (Matt. 13:30). A disciple lives a sanctified life—a life that is set apart for God in anticipation of this promise and the hope of eternal preservation.

CHAPTER 8

DEVELOPING A MINISTERIAL IDENTITY

And the evil spirit answered and said, "Jesus I know, and Paul I know; but who are you?" (Acts 19:15)

The importance of a strong identity has been established by noted psychologists. Erik Erikson, for example, has done significant research about youth and identity. After studying all the stages of life and the unique problems of each life stage across different cultures, Erikson claimed the most significant issue for young people is the question of identity.

It is very important to know who we are. Discipleship is a journey of discovery of who we are in Jesus Christ. Unfortunately, while the church is neglecting its commission to make disciples, various cults and groups are taking advantage of this vacuum. Millions are turning to cults, unwholesome meditations, and charlatans of all kinds to find their identity. The formation of a Christian identity is an essential part of discipleship. It is God's will for us to know who we are, and He has given us insights regarding this matter in the Bible.

Disciples Are Children of God

Christians have been born again into a new identity, which they must discover. They have been adopted into God's family. They are heirs of the Father and joint heirs with Jesus Christ. They have the privilege of calling almighty God by the familiar term *Abba* (Father): "The Spirit itself beareth witness with our spirit, that we are the children of God: and if children, then heirs; heirs of God, and joint-heirs with Christ" (Rom. 8:16–17 KJV). John noted, "But as many as received him, to them gave he power to become the sons of God, even to them that believe on his name" (John 1:12 KJV), and then he added, "Beloved, now are we the sons of God" (1 John 3:2 KJV). Disciples need to know they belong to the greatest family on earth and they can say, "I am a child of God!"

Disciples Are Sinners Saved by the Grace of God

Christians must never assume they are somehow superior to their fellow human beings. They are, of course, children of God, and yet they remain sinners saved by the grace of God, sinners forgiven and cleansed by the blood of Jesus. The apostle Paul was always conscious of his status as a saved sinner. He wrote to Timothy: "This is a faithful saying, and worthy of all acceptation, that Christ Jesus came into the world to save sinners; of whom I am chief. Howbeit . . . I obtained mercy" (1 Tim. 1:15–16 KJV).

Paul reminded the Christians at Ephesus about their status as saved sinners: "For by grace are ye saved through faith; and that not of yourselves: it is the gift of God" (Eph. 2:8 KJV). The mystery of the gospel is that we are forgiven sinners who are called to become saints, "set-apart ones." We are not living a sinful life now by the grace of God, but we are aware of our past and are grateful for what God has done for us in Jesus Christ and what we have received by faith. We are saved sinners who now live "as becometh saints" (Eph. 5:3 KJV).

Disciples Are Citizens of Heaven

A person born in a particular country is a citizen of that country. Christians are born into the kingdom of heaven, and this makes them citizens of that kingdom. Some countries used to sell citizenship; one had to pay a large amount of money to purchase citizenship. We could never afford to pay the cost of our heavenly citizenship, but Jesus paid the price for our citizenship at Calvary and offered this purchased citizenship free of charge to those who believe in Him. This costly citizenship is God's gift to us.

Even though he was proud to be a citizen of the great Roman Empire, Paul was not ashamed to proclaim that "our citizenship is in heaven" (Phil. 3:20). He said, "Now therefore ye are no more strangers and foreigners, but fellowcitizens with the saints, and of the household of God" (Eph. 2:19 KJV). This new citizenship in heaven makes the followers of Jesus strangers and aliens on earth. A disciple's life, manners, and even speech should reflect this foreign citizenship. A disciple of Jesus has a holy accent.

The church fathers tell us the Old Testament saints anticipated this "foreign" citizenship:

> By faith he [Abraham] sojourned in the land of promise, as in a strange country, dwelling in tabernacles with Isaac and Jacob . . . for he looked for a city which hath foundations, whose builder and maker is God. . . . These all died in faith, not having received the promises, but having seen them afar off, and were persuaded of them, and embraced them, and confessed that they were strangers and pilgrims on the earth. . . . they desire a better country, that is, an heavenly. (Heb. 11:9–10, 13, 16 KJV)

Disciples Are Servants

The disciples of Jesus are not to be just members of the crowd that come to see miracles. They are called to stay with the Master, even after the multitude leaves. Disciples are God's servants. They have not chosen Him; He has chosen them. It is a privilege to serve Him. Jesus said, "If any man serve me, let him follow me; and where I am, there shall also my servant be: if any man serve me, him will my father honour" (John 12:26 KJV).

Paul wrote to the Colossians about the behavior expected of Jesus' disciples: "And whatsoever ye do, do it heartily, as to the Lord, and not unto men; knowing that of the Lord ye shall receive the reward of the inheritance: for ye serve the Lord Christ" (Col. 3:23–24 KJV). Disciple makers must provide opportunities for believers to discover their true identities in

Christ. The discipleship curriculum must consider this need a priority, because disciples need a strong sense of identity to live as whole people in a broken world.

All disciples of Jesus are called to serve. Some are called to full-time Christian service. We call them vocational ministers. All disciples are called to be disciple makers and are ministers in the making. Ordained ministers are mature disciples with advanced spiritual growth who develop a more defined identity as ministers.

Discipleship and Ordained Ministry

Donald E. Messer shared several contemporary images of ordained ministry. He believes that ministry today suffers from being perceived through stereotypical images.[47] He stated that many people consider ministers either hired hands or super saints. These images distort the true meaning of ministry as a gift of God to all God's people. These contemporary images of ministry Messer identified are summarized below.

1. Minister as wounded healer in the community of the compassionate. In this view, the church is the compassionate community, and ministers bring healing to others as wounded people on their own journey toward wholeness.
2. Minister as servant leader in a servant church. Here the church is a community of servants, and ministers are servant leaders.
3. Minister as political mystic in a prophetic community. This view sees the church as a community called to speak prophetically to the world, and ministers are

political mystics who do not conform to the world and its systems.

4. Minister as enslaved liberator of the rainbow church. The church in this view is a multicultural global community that stands for the liberation of all people from all forms—social, political, economic, etc.—of enslavement. Ministers are liberators who are themselves slaves (servants) of Christ.
5. Minister as practical theologian in a postdenominational church. The church here is not only nondenominational; it is a postdenominational community of faith. Ministers are practical theologians who empower lay leaders to do the work of the ministry.
6. Minister as good shepherd in a global village. The world has become a global village; the church is the flock of God. Ministers are shepherds who feed and lead the sheep.

According to William Willimon, a graduate of my alma mater, Yale Divinity School, and well-known Methodist bishop who served as dean of the chapel at Duke University, other contemporary images of ministry include the following:

1. Minister as media personality
2. Minister as political negotiator
3. Minister as therapist
4. Minister as manager
5. Minister as resident activist
6. Minister as preacher
7. Minister as servant leader[48]

Willimon proposed that ministry should be countercultural, since according to Scripture, ministers are aliens and exiles (1 Pet. 2:11). He believes that ministry must recover its classical forms of preaching, teaching, evangelizing, and healing as it responds to the critical needs of the church and the world.

Willimon sees ministry as an act of God and of the church. He believes to be a pastor is to be intimately connected to the church; thus, ministry is a difficult vocation. He defines ordination as an act of Christ and His church, for service to Christ and His church. According to Willimon, ordination arises from above, as a gift of the Holy Spirit (2 Tim. 1:6). It also arises from below, from the church's need for leadership. The *process* of being ordained transforms and forms those who are to serve as priests for their position within a community of priests. It sets those apart who are to serve as examples. Ordination is an act of collegiality, made effective through the laying on of hands (1 Cor. 3:5–9).

Some Highlights

How does the Bible define ordained ministry? I provided a detailed answer to this question in my 2017 book *Spirit-Led Ministry in the Twenty-First Century.* Let us review some highlights here.

Scripture defines ministry as being a coworker with God, carrying out His purposes in the world (John 4:34; 2 Cor. 6:1). Almighty God chooses to depend on fragile human beings to complete His work of restoration, reconciliation, and redemption in this fallen world. Ministry is, therefore, doing God's will in the world. But before God's will can be carried out, it must be sought in prayer. Ministry, then, is seeking God's will in prayer and doing His will through one's life (1 John 2:17).

Ordained ministers are not expected to carry out all of the practical aspects of ministry. God gave apostles, prophets, evangelists, pastors, and teachers for the equipping of the believers to do the work of the ministry, according to Ephesians 4:12. To a large degree, ministry is simply equipping and enabling other believers to fulfill the multiple ministries of God's church. The ultimate purpose of ministry is, therefore, to produce disciples who minister. Although not all are called to the office of ministry, all believers are called to minister. True ministry is enabling others to serve in the name of Jesus by edifying, equipping, and helping them to grow. This is the work and ultimate purpose of discipleship.

Jesus is the best model of a pastor and shepherd. In *Jesus the Pastor*, John W. Frye identified the characteristics of Jesus as a model shepherd.[49] Jesus had a strong sense of identity; He knew who He was and what He was called to do. This sense of identity enabled Him to focus on His destiny and purpose. Significantly, Jesus did not depend on His ministerial performance to settle His identity; His father affirmed Him before He performed the first miracle, saying, "You are my Son, whom I love; with you I am well pleased" (Luke 3:22 NIV). Jesus' identity was not based on performance, rather it was rooted in Father God. Many ministers fall into the trap of performance-based identity, but a biblical model of ministry is anchored in God and in His call on the minister's life.

The Spirit of the Lord was upon Jesus to preach the good news. He was God in the flesh to the degree that those around him could say, "We beheld His glory" (John 1:14). As a shepherd, He had a compassionate heart. He went about His Father's work, ministering to the oppressed. He was spiritually disciplined, committed to a community, and willing to tell the truth at all costs. He was not afraid of the devil, but He took the power of evil seriously. He also shared authority with His disciples; He knew that sharing His authority did not diminish it.

Theologically speaking, a minister is an incarnational presence of Christ. According to the apostle Paul, a Christian's body is "the temple of the Holy Spirit" (1 Cor. 6:19); that is, the Holy Spirit dwells in each believer. Incarnational presence represents the idea that when ministers are present with someone in need, they bring the presence of Christ in some inexplicable way. While ministry involves both being and doing, the concept of the incarnational presence represents both being and doing at the same time. Being present fully with someone in the name of Jesus is a ministerial practice. This ministry has great potential, especially when we are working with individuals who are suffering and hurting. You may have noticed that people in pain do not remember the words of ministers as much as they remember their presence.

The incarnational presence is a way of communicating Christian hope. Paul's words in Colossians undergird this idea: "Christ in you, the hope of glory" (Col. 1:27). A minister practicing the incarnational presence is living with the realization that just being with a suffering person can help bring peace, hope, and healing. Authentic Christian presence can be a healing experience.

One may conclude that Paul was seeking the incarnational presence when he requested Timothy to "come before winter" (2 Tim. 4:21). His longing to be with members of various faith communities as expressed in his letters (Rom. 1:11; Phil. 2:24) point out the value he placed on being present. In this day of virtual reality and cyberpresence, ministers may want to consider the importance of this ministry of physical presence that Paul highlighted, when writing on papyrus was the latest technology available to him.

In summary, we can say that ministry is one's very being. It is our life itself, as disciples of Jesus Christ who are committed to serve Him full time. It involves being with Jesus and doing whatever He has called us to do. In other words, we can say that ministry involves preaching, teaching, healing, and disciple making. In this sense, ministry is being like Jesus. Being like Jesus means being an incarnational presence of the one who called us. Henri Nouwen saw this as becoming a living reminder of Jesus. Ministry must be done by faith and in the power of the Holy Spirit. Ministry is ongoing discipleship where life transformation is expected to be lifelong.

There are other definitions of ministry that can further clarify the identity of a minister. For instance, according to William A. Clebsch and Charles R. Jaekle,[50] ministry is the work of healing, guiding, sustaining, and reconciling. That means a minister is a healer, guide, sustainer, and reconciler. Similarly, according to Nouwen, a minister is a teacher, preacher, counselor, organizer, and celebrator,[51] and according to Victor Paul Furnish and Ronald H. Sunderland, a minister is a monitor of the community, maintainer of the community, and facilitator of koinonia, celebration, and service.[52] Edward Wimberly, an African American theologian who served for a season as a professor at Oral Roberts University, stated that ministers in the black community are parents, guides, and teachers.

Importance of Ministerial Identity

Developing a strong ministerial identity is vital for effective ministry. As a seminary professor and dean, I have seen the struggle of many graduates who lacked a strong ministerial identity. That is why I began my book *Spiritual Identity and Spirit-Empowered Life* (2017) with the story of the sons of Sceva in the book of Acts who ran into big trouble by trying to minister without having a proper spiritual identity. In this sad and humorous story in Acts 19, the unexpected events show the importance of having a strong and authentic Christian spiritual identity. Let us review the story briefly.

Paul was at Ephesus, where he met some disciples, about twelve men. They had been baptized by John's baptism, in the name of Jesus, so they were not familiar with the Holy Spirit. Paul laid hands on them, and they received the Holy Spirit. It was the beginning of the church in Ephesus.

Paul ministered in and around Ephesus for about two years, preaching, teaching, and healing. "God did extraordinary miracles through Paul, so that even handkerchiefs and aprons that had touched him were taken to the sick, and their illnesses were cured and the evil spirits left them" (Acts 19:11–12 NIV). Many were blessed by Paul's ministry there and believed in Jesus. Others did not accept Christ but were fascinated by the supernatural elements of his ministry and their impact on people. Desiring similar effects on people and seeking the results Paul had in his ministry, some tried to imitate him.

There was a Jewish chief priest named Sceva who had seven sons. These men tried to imitate Paul in a real-life situation and attempted to cast out an evil spirit from a possessed man by saying, "In the name of the Jesus whom Paul preaches, I command you to come out" (v. 13). Seeing nothing happening, they kept repeating the same command. Finally, the evil spirit spoke to them, saying, "Jesus I know, and Paul I know about, but who are you?" (v. 15). They were startled, but that was not the end. Now comes the sad—and humorous—part of the story: "Then the man who had the evil spirit jumped on them and overpowered them all. He gave them such a beating that they ran out of the house naked and bleeding" (v. 16)!

The evil spirit told the sons of Sceva that it knew Jesus and Paul but had no clue who *they* were. In other words, this spirit recognized the identities and the authority of Jesus and His apostle Paul, but it questioned the identities and authority of the sons of Sceva, because they lacked any identity that represented a relationship with Jesus and a connection to the power of the Holy Spirit.

One's spiritual identity represents one's authority and power. Jesus had to face the question of identity on a regular basis. People constantly challenged His identity. In His hometown, they asked, "Is this not the carpenter's son? His mother and brothers are among us" (see Matt. 13:55). In other words, they were trying to ascertain His identity as the source of His authority and power, but His identity was not limited to who His earthly father was or who His mother and brothers were. It was more comprehensive, beyond His earthly family connections and including also His spiritual relationships. Jesus' identity and authority were connected to more sources than His biological roots.

Recall the time when Jesus asked His disciples, "Who do people say the Son of Man is?"

They replied, "Some say John the Baptist; others say Elijah; and still others, Jeremiah or one of the prophets."

"But what about you?" Jesus asked, narrowing the focus of His question. "Who do you say I am?"

Peter replied on behalf of all of them, "You are the Messiah, the Son of the living God."

Jesus then told them that flesh and blood had not revealed this truth to them, but rather His Father in heaven (Matt. 16:13–17). It was a revelation. Jesus wanted them to know His true identity and its horizontal and vertical dimensions.

Jesus knew who He was. He had a strong identity. His identity was not based on His performance. He was already affirmed by His Father before His first miracle. His identity was rooted in God the Father. It was naturally connected to His earthly relationships, but it transcended those; it was rooted deeply in His relationship with His heavenly Father, who had given Him His purpose and destiny, and in the power of the Spirit that was upon Him (Luke 4:18).

Remember when Jesus entered Jerusalem and the people asked, "Who is this?" He had been there many times, but it seems that He was unknown in the holy city. Jesus did not verbally answer their question that day; instead He went to the temple and began to heal the sick. He was answering the question of His identity with His deeds rather than His words. He demonstrated that He was the one with divine authority over the temple. He was not the priest or the high priest, but He was the one who had the authority to cleanse the temple. The blind and the lame came in when Jesus was in the temple, but they did not leave blind or lame. That was the demonstration of His identity and authority; that was His answer to the question, "Who is this?"

Jesus knew who He was. His identity empowered Him to fulfill His purpose and destiny. Knowing who He was and empowered by that knowledge and the anointing of the Holy Spirit, He exercised authority over natural forces, demonic powers, sicknesses, and death (Luke 8). The devil knew that Jesus was the Son of God. He knew that all authority had been given to Jesus. The people missed it on that day in Jerusalem, because He had come riding on a donkey. But the devil did not miss it, and that is clear from the evil spirit's response to the sons of Sceva.

Like Jesus, Paul also had a strong sense of identity. The devil knew him too. Paul's identity gave him and represented in him the authority of an apostle. He talked about being "circumcised on the eighth day, of the people of Israel, of the tribe of Benjamin, a Hebrew of Hebrews; in regard to the law, a Pharisee; as for zeal, persecuting the church; as for righteousness based on the law, faultless" (Phil. 3:5–6 NIV). He had a very strong ethnic identity based on his family and heritage, but while owning that personal identity, he counted all of it a loss and embraced instead his spiritual identity. He knew he was an apostle called, empowered, and sent by God.

He did not apologize for it, but his spiritual identity gave him the authority to say to others without fear, "I charge you" (1 Thess. 5:27; 1 Tim. 5:21), "I urge you" (Acts 27:22; 1 Tim. 6:13), and "Who has bewitched you?" (Gal. 3:1). This strong sense of spiritual identity was behind his supernatural ministry in Ephesus, which the sons of Sceva disastrously tried to imitate.

The chief priest's sons ran into trouble by not being authentic disciples of Jesus. They were not filled with the Holy Spirit, so they were missing the empowerment they needed to cast the spirit out. The evil spirit wound up questioning their identity and overcoming them physically. They had to run for their lives, bleeding and naked.

Spiritual identity matters. Having a strong sense of identity as a member of God's family and as a vessel of the Holy Spirit is very important to living a purposeful and victorious life as a disciple of Jesus and, especially, if you are called, as a full-time Christian minister. For those who are so called, their spiritual identity becomes the foundation of their ministerial identity.

The followers of Jesus who may sense a call to full-time ministry must consider what biblical ministry is as described in this book and seek confirmation of their calling from trustworthy people who have spiritual authority over them. If confirmed internally and externally, they should seek the education and training to match their calling. They should also seek mentoring to grow spiritually and to develop a strong ministerial identity. Discipleship is a journey of faith and formation. Ministers are disciples themselves and sojourners with the faithful. There is no vocation more fulfilling than following God's call to make disciples of all nations.

CHAPTER 9

ADULT EDUCATION (ANDRAGOGY) AND DISCIPLE MAKING

> So why do you worry about clothing? Consider the lilies of the field, how they grow: they neither toil nor spin. (Matt. 6:28)
>
> Then Jesus called a little child to Him, set him in the midst of them, and said, "Assuredly, I say to you, unless you are converted and become as little children, you will by no means enter the kingdom of heaven." (Matt. 18:2–3)

Discipleship is a transformational faith journey of learning and growth. Disciple makers, regardless of their official titles or lack thereof, are educators, mentors, and coaches. Jesus is the best model for a disciple maker. Jesus was a mentor, model, coach, and educator. He commissioned His disciples to make disciples through conversion and education: "Go therefore and make disciples of all the nations, baptizing them in the name of the Father and of the Son and of the Holy Spirit, teaching them to observe all things that I have commanded you; and lo, I am with you always, even to the end of the age" (Matt. 28:19–20). In other words, He called them to imitate Him in His work of disciple making through teaching, coaching, modeling, and mentoring. In this chapter we will consider church-based Christian education as a vehicle of disciple making.

Jesus called His disciples to preach, *teach*, and heal (Matt. 4:23). Preaching alone does not create disciples. Preaching can be one of the tools involved in spiritual formation, but the transformation of lives requires much more than preaching. Preaching can be limited to information sharing, and it requires little from the listeners. Preaching was not the primary means Jesus and Paul used to make disciples. Moving from exerting pressure on disciples to mature to providing opportunities for natural participation in life and learning enhances the discipleship process.

Preaching can produce believers and converts, but conversion is only the entry point to discipleship. An intentional teaching and mentoring ministry is required to develop a mature disciple. Moving from hierarchy to peer relationship, from dialogue to dynamic exchange can help disciples to become disciple makers.

We have already noticed that in this era of user friendliness, seeker focus, and mega-everything, the church today suffers from a major shortage of discipleship. This seems especially true within fellowships where no teaching is deemed necessary beyond the children's Sunday school. While 77 percent of Americans identify as Christian, and 44 percent say they belong to a Christian congregation, only 20 percent show up to worship weekly.[53] Currently, this rate is further decreasing. What's the problem? An increasing number of Christians are cultural Christians, just as many Hindus are cultural Hindus in India.

There are Christians who affirm the Christian confession, but they do not live what they confess. They will claim they "believe," but they do not practice what they believe. They may belong to a church, but they feel no obligation to support the church and participate in its life in a meaningful way. These are church members, spectator Christians, "sloganized" constituents, not engaged disciples.

Cultural Christianity will not produce true followers of Christ. God wants to transform the followers of Jesus to become mature disciples. He is looking for people who have counted the cost of following Christ and do not mind being different from the world in their respective cultures. He wants them to live as citizens of heaven and participants in the kingdom of God.

Discipleship has to be intentional, not accidental. The church must make disciple making a priority—not just crowd gathering. Teaching the Word of God is central to the task of disciple making. God's Word is the disciples' rule book for faith and practice. A community of faith, something much smaller than mega, is needed to develop disciples. It takes the context of a smaller group of believers to develop disciples. Disciples are formed and shaped in smaller communities even in a megachurch. Discipleship can take place in bigger churches and larger ministries, but the actual formational work happens in small groups of committed followers of Jesus who are guided by godly teachers and mentors who are not control freaks.

Every church needs a plan to develop disciples, but it takes more than good intentions. It takes a commitment to provide the teaching and the relationships that are required to make it happen. The Lord's command is not "Gather a crowd" but "Make disciples" (Matt. 28:19)! People of all ages must be discipled. In fact, discipleship should be the direct and implied goal of all church programs, especially Christian education programs.

Discipleship can start at any age. Children and adolescents must be offered intentional discipleship experiences. They need to be discipled through teaching, training, modeling, and mentoring. Teaching must rely on more than the brain of the student to be effective. According to Larry Richards, good teaching must involve understanding, emotions, values, and decisions on the part of the teacher.[54] It takes patience, presence, and persistence to be a good teacher of God's Word. Patience allows a teacher to lovingly accept the student, and presence represents availability without invasion. Persistence means presenting God's truth faithfully. Thus, teaching is more than just talking or letting the students talk, and good teaching extends beyond the classroom or the sanctuary.

EPIC Generation

Teachers should also consider their students' ability to retain information, as illustrated by the following chart:

Percentage of Information Retained	Of What They:
10%	Hear
30%	See
50%	See and Hear
70%	See, Hear, and Say
90%	See, Hear, Say, and Do[55]

If this is the case, pastors and teachers need to do more than talk. Leonard Sweet, in *Post-Modern Pilgrims*, calls students in the postmodern world the EPIC generation: (1) *e*xperiential, (2) *p*articipative, (3) *i*mage-based, and (4) *c*onnected.[56] This means that teachers need to incorporate new methods to enhance learning, such as videos, PowerPoints, dramas, storytelling, and dialogue, in addition to discussions, debates, and group exercises. Stated more technically, learning involves three domains within the student: the affective, the cognitive, and the behavioral (psycho-motor). The *affective* realm primarily involves feelings and emotions; in this area a teacher should aim to create inspiration in the student. The *cognitive* domain involves knowledge and intellect. Students will grow in this area to the degree the teaching content is effective. The *behavioral* area of learning impacts the will and the activities of students, which will manifest in their lifestyle.

Christians in the twenty-first century are called to communicate the gospel to a culture of entertainment, reverse values, violence, and materialism. In order to meet this challenge, pastors and educators need to do more than pursue business as usual. Pastors and teachers must acquire an adequate understanding of how people of all ages learn, and then they must apply that understanding to their discipleship efforts. Competent pastors and teachers are needed to develop disciples of all ages.

The young generation today does not live in a world in which many of their teachers were educated, and the instruction they receive in their secular schools with cutting-edge technology is much different from what their teachers experienced as students. They will not respond well to a "business as usual" type of low-budget Sunday school or Christian education program. Consider the fact that children today are a generation that has access to information without supervision. Previously, young people went to teachers, authority figures, and experts for information. Teachers still need to present information, but much information is available to the students before they meet the teacher. Modern teaching must take this reality into account.

Once upon a time, teaching was conceptualized as pouring information from the teacher, the big bucket, into the pupil, the little bucket. This pedagogical model is outdated. Teachers need to provide more than information; students must also be taught how to apply the information, especially by developing the capability to evaluate the information for truthfulness and faithfulness to the Word of God. Information sharing should not be the only purpose of Sunday schools; transformation of individuals through discipleship should be the ultimate goal. This requires caring pastors and teachers who are willing to be trained in modern teaching methods that consider the true nature of today's learners.

A discussion on effective discipleship through Christian education must begin with two questions. First, what is Christian education? Second, what is the purpose of Christian education? Christian education is a Bible-based, Holy Spirit–empowered, Christ-centered, and mission-driven teaching-learning process. The purpose of Christian education is to guide individuals at all ages and stages of life through contemporary teaching methodologies to help them grow in grace and in the knowledge of the Lord Jesus Christ until Christ is formed in them and they increasingly conform to His image.

This type of transformation does not happen accidentally; it requires a strategy. The teacher should model Jesus Christ, the master educator, and intentionally follow His directive to make disciples. Jesus the master teacher always emphasized the pupil. He was a teacher of great authority and profound simplicity. He taught with definite goals and always started with the pupils' needs. Jesus used a variety of teaching methods, such as questions, discussions, lectures, stories, and teaching aids. There is a need to think creatively to find the contemporary applications of Jesus' methods of teaching, modeling, and mentoring.

Teaching children and youth requires teachers to understand their physical, mental, social, and spiritual characteristics. Physically, children, especially adolescents, deal with bursts of energy and recurring fatigue, because they grow and develop at a rapid pace. Teenagers, for instance, feel awkward about their bodies and their disproportionate growth. They also have keen minds and are often critical of everyone and everything as they begin to evaluate the truth about the world for themselves. Socially, they are greatly influenced by their peers, being in the process of transferring their loyalty from their parents to peers. Although they may act otherwise, teens need acceptance from teachers as they look to younger adults as role models. They are also sincere and serious about their spiritual life and desire to know God but cannot handle long, boring lectures. They prefer learning activities that will enhance their spiritual development through social interactions. Due to these characteristics, adolescents are prime candidates for discipleship training.

Let us consider educating adult believers to become mature disciples. Although Christian conversion is an internal matter, the Christian life displays external evidence. The New Testament documents several individuals whose lives were transformed by an encounter with Jesus. The Samaritan woman who met Jesus at the well was changed by that encounter (John 4:29), and the demoniac Legion who met Jesus received a sound mind (Luke 8:35). Similarly, the despised tax collector Zacchaeus became a philanthropist after he met Jesus in Jericho (Luke 19:8). The story of the Ethiopian eunuch testifies that an encounter with Jesus through the mediation of an evangelist is as powerful as an encounter with Jesus in the flesh. Philip introduced the Ethiopian to Jesus on a desert road in Gaza. The eunuch accepted Christ, was baptized in water in the desert, and went home rejoicing (Acts 8:38)! In the same manner, the jailor who imprisoned Paul and Silas accepted Christ and was instantly impacted. His sins were washed in the baptismal water as he washed the wounds of the apostles (Acts 16:33–34). The largest portion of the New Testament was written by Paul the persecutor who met Jesus and himself became the persecuted.

The change Jesus facilitates in the lives of believers normally manifests in the decisions and choices they make. This is where discipleship training (Christian education) becomes significant. Christian education must equip believers to make decisions and choices that will glorify God. Christians must exhibit a lifestyle that is different from that of non-Christians. Ultimately, our lifestyle is the outcome of the decisions and choices we make. The Bible gives examples of good and bad decisions and choices. For example, Cain made a bad decision to worship with a wrong motive (Gen. 4:8), Esau decided to sell his birthright (Gen. 25:29–34), and Samson chose to confess the secret of his strength to Delilah (Judg. 16:15–17). King Saul decided to disobey God and keep the enemy alive (1 Sam. 15:20), the rich young ruler decided to walk away from the invitation given by Jesus (Matt. 19:16–22), Demas decided to forsake Paul because he chose to love the world (2 Tim. 4:10), and Governor Felix chose not to decide about Christ (Acts 24:24–26).

Thankfully, the Bible presents clear instructions about making healthy decisions and choices. We are to choose unity rather than division (Ps. 133:1). Forgiveness is a better choice than bitterness (Matt. 6:12), and we must choose holiness rather than worldliness (1 Pet. 1:16). Love is a better choice than hatred (1 John 4:7–8), and healing is a better choice than brokenness (John 5:6). Psychologists were not the first ones to say that happiness is a choice; the Bible also teaches this principle. The apostle Paul pleaded with the Philippian believers to choose happiness, saying, "Rejoice in the Lord always. I will say it again: Rejoice!" (Phil. 4:4 NIV). In the Old

Testament, Joshua made the most important decision: "We will serve the LORD" (Josh. 24:15 NIV).

It is the duty of pastors and teachers to raise the level of biblical literacy and Christian discipleship in our churches. Bible college and seminary professors have noticed an astounding level of biblical illiteracy in their incoming students. This appears to be a great problem. The remedy can only spring from the local church, which must raise up disciples of Jesus who know the Word of God to the degree they are able to evaluate their culture and make truly Christian decisions on a daily basis. Sometimes the word *decision* in the evangelical vocabulary is limited to the decision to accept Christ, but we must train people to make God-honoring decisions and choices throughout their lives. The church must equip believers to make morally right decisions through competent and Spirit-led disciple making.

The church is called to make disciples of all nations by teaching them to obey everything Jesus commanded (Matt. 28:20). This requires adequate planning, preparation, and commitment of resources to help Christians "grow in the grace and knowledge of our Lord" (2 Pet. 3:18). Without a learning process, one cannot grow, develop, and transform. A healthy church is a learning community, and all members of the community, including pastors, must become lifelong learners, disciples, and disciple makers.

Churches of the twenty-first century need a Bible-based, Holy Spirit–empowered teaching-learning-transforming process that leads to discipleship and spiritual formation. The ultimate purpose of such a program, aimed at all ages, will be to make mature disciples who will be imitators of the master teacher, Jesus Christ. Unfortunately, in many places, the ministry of teaching has been reduced in priority, and in some cases fully eliminated for grown-ups in favor of gatherings for worship and celebration. Even in churches where an educational ministry is available to adults, the methods used to teach and train them are often classic pedagogy, not andragogy (adult education). Pedagogy's focus (like pediatrics in medicine) is children, not adults. The relatively new field of study called adult education (andragogy) focuses on the best educational practices that contribute to adult learning. Disciple makers must pay attention to this matter.

Andragogy

The last part of the twentieth century witnessed the growth of the field known as adult education. Malcolm S. Knowles is considered the father of the adult education movement. Known as *andragogy* (learning of adults), as opposed to *pedagogy* (learning of children), this field studies adult learners.[57] Although it can be said that good pedagogy techniques would also be effective as andragogy, there are some unique aspects of adult education that do not fully apply to children. For instance, Knowles suggests there are five assumptions of adult education that should be taken seriously by teachers of adults.

Assumptions

About	***Pedagogy***	***Andragogy***
Concept of the learner	Dependent	Self-directing

Role of learner's experience	Not sufficient as a resource	Rich resource for learning
Readiness to learn	Uniform by age, etc.	Develops from life tasks
Orientation to learning	Subject-centered	Problem-centered
Motivation	By external rewards or punishment	Internal incentives or curiosity[58]

By considering Knowles's perspective, pastors and teachers will be able to avoid teaching adults as if they were children. Disciple makers are more than individuals who provide information; they must become guides and mentors to adult disciples.

The sole purpose of some teachers is to enable students to commit information to rote memory. A teacher who instructs and tests based on this goal only measures the student's ability to memorize. Although it is a good thing to memorize the Word of God, according to Benjamin Bloom, memorization is the lowest level of cognitive activity. Bloom lists six levels of learning, ranging from the lowest to the highest:

1. Knowledge: Student is able to recall.
2. Comprehension: Student is able to explain the information.
3. Application: Student can use the information in a meaningful way.
4. Analysis: Student can see the relationship between concepts.

5. Synthesis: Student is able to combine ideas and see the bigger picture.
6. Evaluation: The student is able to make informed judgments.[59]

According to Raymond Wlodkowski, effective teachers of adults are good facilitators who exhibit the following four characteristics. First, they have *expertise* in the field of teaching. For example, a Bible teacher must have a good knowledge of the Word of God. Second, good facilitators have *empathy* toward their students. Empathy helps teachers present the material with a special concern for the needs of the learners. Good facilitators are *enthusiastic* about their students, the subject, and the teaching-learning process. Finally, good facilitators possess *clarity* of thought and presentation.[60]

Effective facilitators also model what they teach and act as expert resource people who know their subject area well. They must be good counselors who are interested in the life challenges and spiritual issues of their students.

Ultimately, good teachers and mentors want to move their adult students from a dependent position to a self-directed position where they can become teachers. This requires teachers to frequently change their role from coaches to salespeople, to facilitators, and to consultants and companions. The Foundation for Critical Thinking presents the following tactics for promoting active learning in a group of adults:[61]

1. Have students summarize what has been taught in their own words.
2. Elaborate on what has been said.

3. Relate the issue being discussed to the life experiences of the students.
4. Give examples to clarify and support what is said.
5. Show connections between related concepts.
6. Let students state the question at issue.
7. Let students restate instructions in their own words.
8. Describe to what extent the students' current point of view is similar or different from the teacher's or other's.
9. Put a response in written form.
10. Write down the most pressing question on the students' mind.
11. Discuss any of the above with partners.

It appears that adults learn best when teachers use methods that:

1. Reduce anxiety.
2. Let students show what they know.
3. Give clear directions.
4. Show the relevance of the lesson.
5. Value the accuracy of responses or activities over the speed of response.
6. Repeat the information and allow deep processing.
7. Pace the lesson presentation at a reasonable speed.
8. Avoid distractions and interference.
9. Give both visual and auditory stimuli.
10. Make sure students are physically comfortable in the classroom.

The teaching ministry of the church has not matched the challenges of the postmodern world. Postmodern society imposes so many major issues on individuals that they clearly require more resources than the ability to quote a verse or two. Individuals must be taught to make decisions and abide by them as kingdom citizens in this world. In this way believers can develop the capacity to make internal decisions about their lifestyles.

Jesus must become the model teacher in the pulpit and the classroom. Several writers have identified Jesus' qualities as a teacher. Jesus, as a teacher, was a man of love, excitement, and optimism. He was an approachable teacher who believed in an informal way of teaching. Jesus taught as one with authority yet with profound simplicity. Jesus emphasized the pupil, not Himself, and He always started with the student's needs. Jesus was not a boring teacher, because He believed in using a variety of teaching methods, such as questions, discussions, lectures, and stories. He often incorporated everyday objects as teaching tools.

Good teachers must make room for the Holy Spirit to move in their classroom because the Spirit is the principal teacher who will lead everyone to truth. The ultimate truth is Jesus, who described Himself as the way, the truth, and the life. The Holy Spirit helps both teachers and learners, and He prepares the environment for the proper transmission of truth. First, the Holy Spirit enables teachers to understand the truth; then He opens the mind of students to receive the truth. Without the assistance of the Holy Spirit, the impact of teaching is limited.

The purpose of Christian education is not just the simple transfer of information. Christian education as disciple making is transformational. Studying God's Word involves transformational change in knowledge (cognitive area), attitude (affective area), and behavior (psychomotor area). Instead of conforming to the world, God's people are called to be transformed by the renewing of their minds. This transformational change, made possible with the help of the Holy Spirit, should be the expected outcome of teaching and discipling.

CHAPTER 10

IMPACTING THE WORLD BY IMPLEMENTING THE TRUE MISSION OF THE CHURCH

Go therefore and make disciples of all the nations, baptizing them in the name of the Father and of the Son and of the Holy Spirit, teaching them to observe all things that I have commanded you; and lo, I am with you always, even to the end of the age. (Matt. 28:19–20)

Some years ago, I attended a conference of directors of DMin degree programs in the United States and Canada sponsored by the Association of Doctor of Ministry Education (ADME). A presentation was made about the traditional paradigms of churches in North America. We learned there were five paradigms, but the presenters exhorted us to teach DMin students to develop a sixth paradigm "to do church." First, let's review the five models as they were described at the conference.

Church Paradigms

The first paradigm is called the Soul-Winning Church. This church focuses on evangelism. The pastor sees his role as an evangelist, and the church members see themselves as "bringers of people." The worship style is traditional evangelistic, and the evidence of success is the number of converts.

The second type is called the Experiential Church. This church emphasizes worship, that is, charismatic worship. The pastor's main role is worship leader, and the church members are the audience. The measure of success is the "experience" or "the Spirit."

The third paradigm is called the Family Reunion Church. The pastor is the host, and the church members are family members. The worship style is evangelical, and the measure of success is "preserving our roots."

The fourth paradigm is the Classroom Church. Here, the pastor is a teacher, and the church members are students. The worship style is educational, basically pedagogical. The measure of success is edification through expository preaching.

The fifth model is called the Social Gospel Church. The pastor is a reformer, and the church members are activists. The worship style is liturgical, and the measure of success is social change.

It was interesting that there was no discussion of a paradigm called the Disciple-Making Church. Consideration of a Christ-centered church that impacts the world through discipleship and spiritual formation became obvious at this conference. So we were properly reminded that a sixth model synthesizing all the aspects of the existing paradigms was needed. This model would be called a Renewing Church or simply a Disciple-Making Church. The pastor is a disciple maker and equipper in this paradigm, and the church members are ministers. Worship can be traditional, contemporary, and/or charismatic. But the measure of success would be transformed lives, spiritual maturity, and the number of disciple makers. Shouldn't all churches be this type?

In this book, we have closely examined discipleship and disciple making from both biblical and theological perspectives. We have established the vital importance of practicing the ministry of disciple making in local churches across the world. But what are the practical steps involved in making disciples in our local congregations?

The Local Church

Once again, we must begin with the Bible's teaching about the local church. The church is not only a resource for disciple making but also the major context of the disciple-making ministry. The church, according to the Word of God, is not a man-made organization. It has an organizational dimension that should be run in a businesslike fashion, but the church is primarily (1) a building and field (1 Cor. 3:9), (2) a planting and garden (1 Cor. 3:6), (3) a vineyard and flock (1 Cor. 9:7), (4) a temple (1 Cor. 3:16), (5) a household (Gal. 6:10), (6) an olive tree (Rom. 11:17, 24), and (7) the people of God (1 Pet. 2:9). Theologically speaking, the church is (1) the community called by God, (2) a people called to be saints, (3) a band of faithful people, (4) the assembly of servants, (5) the family of the children of God, (6) the commonwealth of kings and priests, (7) a body with many members, and (8) an eschatological community. This church as a community is the crucible for making disciples. Individuals are transformed in this community. As they are transformed, the community itself experiences continuing transformation.

The church of Jesus Christ is more than an organization; it is a living organism. All living organisms must grow, develop, and maintain their health. But what does a healthy church look like?

A Healthy Church

In Gerkin's book, *An Introduction to Pastoral Care*,[62] he examines the congregation as a community of faith and describes the five characteristics of a healthy congregation. I believe all churches can benefit from examining themselves and considering these characteristics.

First, according to Gerkin, a healthy congregation is a community of language. Second, a healthy congregation is a community of memory. Third, a healthy congregation is a community of inquiry. Fourth, a healthy congregation is a community of mutual care. Finally, a healthy congregation is a community of mission. In other words, a healthy church must be a Christ-centered community of language, memory, inquiry, mutual care, and mission.

1. A Community of Language

By the term *community of language*, Gerkin is not talking about any particular native language; he is talking about the language of the Bible and the images and metaphors contained in the Bible. According to Gerkin, we must become a community that uses biblical language, images, and metaphors. We must see the Word of God forming and informing our worldview.

The Bible is the history of a people called by God to follow Him. It contains the history of the people of God in migration as well as exile. Migration and exile are two different things. Exiles are forced to live the way they do. Migrants are volunteers. Modern Americans are migrants and the offspring of migrants. According to biblical language, we must see ourselves as aliens and pilgrims in this world who are looking for a city whose builder and maker is God.

2. A Community of Memory

A community of memory is one that remembers its past, especially the ways in which the Lord has brought it thus far. We are told not to forget all His benefits (Ps. 103:2). It offends God when His people forget His mercies.

We must not forget our past and what the Lord has done for us. Moreover, we should teach our children about our past, lest they forget their roots. This means we must find ways to keep the memory of God's dealings with us alive. We need preachers and teachers who can remind us of our past as well as take us to a better future.

3. A Community of Inquiry

Adult students tell me their own communities do not encourage them to continue their education. This is true especially of those who study theology and ministry. Somehow we think only young people should be learners. We ignore the fact that the whole world is moving to the concept of lifelong learning. This is especially true in North America. All major corporations are supporting their employees in the quest for lifelong learning. The world is changing so fast and new information is generated so rapidly that, unless one remains a student for life, it is impossible to excel in one's field. The old "Sunday school is for kids" mentality must change in our churches. Being ignorant does not glorify God.

The average American adult changes jobs several times within a lifetime. Student days cannot be limited to young adulthood. There are so many user-friendly ways in which adults can learn now. We must take advantage of these. A typical seminary student in North America is in his or her thirties. We must not discourage adult learners. Learning is the best form of investment.

We must get beyond the fear of education. We must become an inquiring community—inquiring about the profitable things of this world and the things of God.

4. A Community of Mutual Care

The church must become a truly caring community. Being so caught up in seeking our own well-being, we tend to neglect the needs of others. To ensure a good future for all of us, we must find ways to care for one another. Let us first seek the kingdom of God, that is, the well-being of others in the name of Christ. God has promised, as we seek His kingdom, that all the other things we need shall be added to us (Matt. 6:33).

Many churches are growing but are not providing mutual caring for their members. A healthy church is a caring community. We must all become caregivers by being trained to assist others who are struggling with various challenges.

5. A Community of Mission

Christians need a missions strategy that is bigger than themselves. We have been too shortsighted in our missionary strategy. Short-term missions are definitely in God's plan; however, we should not assume God has exempted us from long-term commitments. I believe we need to be involved in the Great Commission locally and globally. The world needs the good news we carry. The issue of discipleship is related to this matter, because a disciple is a learner (educational), a family member (relational), and a missionary (missional).

A healthy church is the best context for disciple making. While parachurch organizations can promote discipleship, they cannot replace the church. Even in the post-Covid world, the church stands unique in its mission and function. It is called to be a safe place of learning (education), belonging (relationship), and transformational mission (missional).

Undriven Disciple Making

Discipling and disciple making should not be just another program of the church periodically driven from the pulpit. It should become the primary business that governs everything else in the church. I am not a fan of anything driven in the church as a program. Drivenness does not produce healthy disciples. Hyperventilating saints who are driven by legalistic rules, regulations, and competitive assignments do not really produce world-impacting disciples. The post-Covid world requires something different, something that is calmer, Spirit led, involving love and care, utilizing teaching and modeling, prayerful and nonobsessive, transparent, and having minimum hierarchy.

Disciple making is a slow-paced, high-touch ministry, especially at the early stages of the effort. This approach moves in the opposite direction of today's high-tech society, which is fast and superficial. As a professor emeritus of pastoral care, I believe in disciple making and church growth, not through compulsion and drivenness, but through love, care, and nurture. Let me explain the aspect of caring in the work of disciple making, because it seems to be the missing element in many forty-day driven programs.

Disciple Making and Caring

Instead of being driven by a compulsion to change people through task-oriented legalism, disciple makers should start with a caring heart for the lost and the newly found. They also need to develop some caregiving skills. I have met my share of people who have been wounded by disciple makers who are themselves wounded. No, one does not need to be a perfect person or a super Christian or a skilled therapist to be an outstanding disciple maker, but one has to balance one's task orientation and relationship orientation in this divine project.

I define caring as loving and loving as giving because "God so loved the world that He gave." In the work of disciple making, giving means giving of oneself, which translates to giving of one's time and attention. I see time as the currency of life in all our human transactions.

Some enter the ministry of disciple making assuming it is strictly a teaching ministry. But we have seen that discipling is not just transferring information; it is sharing our life at a level of transparency even as we are teaching, coaching, and modeling. It is a ministry of self-giving. Unfortunately, we cannot give what we do not have. To give care, we must receive care. To give care regularly, we must receive care regularly. God does not expect us to give from our emptiness: "Freely you have received, freely give" (Matt. 10:8). Sometimes our caregiving is poor because our care receiving was poor. We must receive care from our loving God, our caring family, and the caring members of the body of Christ. Every pastor needs a pastor. This is true of all disciple makers.

Disciple makers must be genuine individuals, because discipleship requires authentic relationships. A good disciple maker has a balanced self-image. People with poor self-esteem relate poorly. Conversely, people who think too highly of themselves also relate poorly. Often such people cover up their poor self-esteem with a "holier than thou" facade.

A good disciple maker has the gift of discernment, which is the biblical equivalent of "knowing" or "understanding." Webster defines *discernment* as "the quality of being able to grasp and comprehend what is obscure." This is an important gift that will help to assess needs and encourage progress in the people we are discipling.

Patience is another requirement. True patience helps disciple makers to be participants in the disciple's journey of growth.

Honesty is another important qualification for disciple makers. Disciple makers should be honest with themselves first, and then honest with others as well. To speak the truth in love is neither judgment nor rejection. It is a true form of caring and instruction. God is in the business of making *new* people, not just *nice* people. We cannot help to renew people unless we learn to tell the truth in love. Speaking the truth in love means telling the truth to someone about themselves in such a way that they can tell the truth about themselves to themselves.

A spirit of humility is another desired qualification. Being humble enough to listen and learn from even a novice makes us better disciple makers. There is always something we can learn or need to learn from the person we are discipling. Receiving feedback with appreciation is humility, and humility produces a teachable spirit. A humble and teachable spirit is conducive to the further growth of the disciple maker.

Successful disciple makers are individuals who find fulfillment in being a member of a group or team. Anyone driven to be a religious superman or a theological wonder woman would not make an impactful disciple maker. Persons who are restrained in their use of God's name as their authority for the things they say or do are more effective in disciple making. People who frequently and casually mention God as inspiring everything they say and do seek to create the impression they have a superior communication with God. Such individuals try to bolster their credibility by inappropriately invoking the authority of God on essential and nonessential matters. By doing so, they put everyone who disagrees with them in the position of challenging God. Often, ordinary people exhibiting this pattern are plagued with low self-esteem. They fear their opinions may not be accepted, so they present them as pronouncements from God.

The following ten characteristics of good pastoral caregivers will suit good disciple makers also.

1. They are relational people.
2. They are good listeners.
3. They accept people as they are, even when they cannot endorse certain beliefs or practices.
4. They pay attention to verbal and nonverbal expressions.
5. They do not label people.
6. They know the difference between conviction and condemnation (conviction is the work of the Holy Spirit).
7. They do not misuse God's name for authority.
8. They keep confidentiality.
9. They differentiate between their needs and the needs of others.
10. They are teachable people.

I focus so much on the required qualities of the disciple maker because Jesus used an intentionally relational method to make disciples. People whose priority is task completion are not the best disciple makers. Even when one acknowledges the differences in the approaches of Jesus and Paul regarding discipleship, one can see the common factor in both these models is the emphasis on caring relationships.

An Honest Self-Evaluation

I invite all pastors and church leaders to do an honest evaluation of the ministry of their church. This will undoubtedly result in an evaluation of the personal ministry of everyone involved. The following are eight areas of church ministry and some questions to evaluate a church as an organization and organism:

1. Mission: Does our church have a mission statement? What does the current mission statement of the church say? Does it clearly relate to the Great Commission? Is our mission statement too generic? Is the mission of the church stated publicly at the gatherings of the church? What is our church known for?
2. Objective: What are the expected outcomes of our current ministry efforts? Is our only objective horizontal church growth? Is disciple making an intentionally expected objective? Is the spiritual formation of members our objective? Do we truly expect to make disciples of Jesus? Is our objective increased membership or intentional discipleship? Do we have any reliable way to measure the spiritual growth and transformation of our people? What will our members look like or act like if the mission of our church is fully realized?
3. Programs: What are the weekly, monthly, yearly programs of our church? Are these programs consistent with the mission of our church? How many programs are sustained by simply pumping them from the pulpit? How many programs should be given decent burials? Do our programs entertain or edify? What new efforts need to be initiated considering the amended (if needed) mission statement of our church? Do we keep doing the same thing in the same way without looking at its

effectiveness? Do we have small groups functioning in the church? What are they named? Cell groups? Care groups? Do they function as care groups or didactic groups? Are the group leaders given adequate training in caring or teaching? Is there spiritual abuse going on in the groups? Is there a group of group leaders for accountability? Do we have a Christian education program? What percentage of our people are involved in it? What percentage of our people are involved in anything more than weekly attendance? What demographic is neglected in our church? Children who do not pay? Youth? Singles? Elderly? Poor? Silent majority?

4. Organization: How is our church organized? Is the running of the church based on the publicly stated version (official organizational chart) or some other way? Is the focus of the organization to make fully committed followers of Jesus? What level of awareness do the people at different levels of the organization have regarding the mission of the church as it relates to disciple making?
5. Staffing: What type of professional (clergy) and nonprofessional staff do we have? Who is paid and who is not? What is the percentage of active members who are active in disciple making? What new staffing (paid or volunteer) is needed to implement disciple making in our church? Who holds power in our church? Are the power brokers interested in disciple making?
6. Facilities: Do we have adequate facilities for our programs? Are there physical hindrances to beginning

a discipleship program in our church? Do we have more real estate than we need? Is real estate a help or a hindrance to the church's ministry? Are the facilities adequately used? How can our real estate help disciple making in our area?

7. Finances: Where is the church's money really going? Does our church's budget support disciple making as the mission of the church? What percentage of the budget is used just for maintenance of the members? What percentage of the budget is used to maintain real estate? What will change in the finances of the church if discipleship becomes the main business of our church? What can be done if implementing the true mission of the church reduces the church's revenue?
8. Output: Is our church like the proverbial shoe factory that does not produce any shoes? Does our church produce disciples of Jesus who are growing spiritually? What level of life transformation do we observe in the people who attend our worship services and/or Christian education ministries? What potential changes will make truly transformed and transforming lives the output of our church?

Embracing a Mega Change

It has been pointed out that intentionality is the most important element of discipleship. Before any plan is implemented, the church must declare its priority and reestablish its intentionality regarding disciple making *and* count the cost. Church leadership must recognize that the church changes the moment it decides to become all about disciple making. Buildings, budget, and attendance (the usual measures of success) will no longer be the main measures of success. This will be a megachange in the thinking of most church leaders and members. Pastors do not find this an easy step to take.

Peter Scazzero acknowledges the threat pastors feel at this point, but based on his experience as a senior pastor, he advises pastors to face their fears and take a step of faith. He confesses he was not a happy volunteer to begin a deeper life as a disciple and disciple-making pastor. "The most important focus is not to change your church," he said, "but to allow Christ to change you." Scazzero confessed his wife had to help him to face himself. One day she said, "Pete, I think the issue is courage, your courage. . . . It is hard to make the changes needed. All I know is that you are in the position to do it, but you aren't doing it. . . . I think this is about you."[63] This loving confrontation helped him to begin a journey of transformation that impacted his church's leadership team first and eventually his congregation. This transition changed four areas of his personal life: prayer, rest, work, and relationships.[64] He gives this advice to pastors and church leaders who wish to change the ministry paradigm in their churches: "If you can work on yourself, then as you interact with others, the church will change. In short, if you do the hard work of allowing God to change you, the whole system will change."[65]

We have seen that a tool, a plan, and a process are required to promote discipleship. Decisions must be made about these matters appropriate to each context. Bible study, prayer, spiritual disciplines (prayer, fasting, etc.) can be considered tools.

Jesus-focused discipleship considers the Bible as the major tool and required curriculum. Bible study cannot be limited to pulpit preaching; there must be time to study the Bible systematically in a complementary way to weekly preaching. Spiritual formation is the outcome of God's activity in an individual through His Spirit and the Word. Disciple makers need to be aware of the three activities involved in their ministry: the disciple maker's activity, the activity of God, and the activity of disciples in terms of their response to the disciple maker, God, and His Word.

The next step is recruitment of candidates to initiate a discipleship program. Recruiting the initial group of candidates for discipleship must be done prayerfully. Bobby Harrington and Josh Patrick's book *The Disciple-Maker's Handbook* (2017)[66] is a good resource for this step. They recommend the following: (1) listen to the congregation and individuals at a deeper level, (2) recruit qualified individuals, (3) prepare the congregation and the members, (4) get ready to engage the cohort, and (5) release them. These are the qualifications of the best candidates: faithful, available, teachable, and reliable individuals. Remember, the objective of the effort is to develop people who will follow Jesus, will be changed by Jesus, and are committed to the mission of Jesus. As we study the Word, listen to the Spirit, and obey the Spirit within healthy and accountable relationships, we are changed to change the world.

Francis Chan provides an outstanding curriculum for discipleship.[67] He recommends starting with three questions: What is a disciple? How do we become disciples? What is the cost of discipleship? According to Chan, teaching individuals how to study the Bible is most important. Teach them to study not because of guilt but to learn about God, about ourselves, and about our world. Ultimately, studying the Bible must help us to live godly lives, facilitate our relationship with God, prepare us to fulfill God's mission, and approach the mind of God. Chan recommends we not study the Bible for interpretation and logical conclusions alone, but to study the Word of God devotionally, obediently, and faithfully for transformation. He presents an interesting concept: following the Bible's storyline from creation to the end of all things.

Greg Ogden recommends a four-part curriculum. The first part addresses these issues: What is discipling? Who is a disciple? How does a disciple grow in Christ on a daily basis? What is the place of the Bible in a disciple's life and quiet time? What is prayer? What is the primary purpose of the church?

Ogden's second part deals with the following questions: Who is the disciple's God? What is humanity? What broke the relationship between God and humanity? What is God's response to our distrust and disobedience? How did Christ reconcile God and us? How are the benefits of the cross transferred to our lives? What is the greatest benefit we receive from our new standing with God?

The third part of the curriculum addresses these concerns: How are we empowered to follow Christ? What is the role of the Holy Spirit in transforming us into the image of Christ? How are we to grow in the knowledge of Christ? What is the authenticating mark to the unbelieving world that we are followers of Jesus? How is sacrificial love expressed among those broken by the world? How does the world come to know the love and justice of Jesus Christ?

The final part deals with these topics: How does Jesus continue to make Himself known? How can we know what our part is in the body of Christ? What opposition can disciples expect and what resources are available to combat this opposition? How are disciples transformed into the likeness of Christ? What is our role in discipling others? What should be disciples' attitude to money?

Spiritual disciplines as described by Richard Foster can be effective tools of formation. According to Foster, spiritual disciplines are those practices that put us in the presence of God where we can have intimate relationship with Him. Ogden points out that Christ is formed in us when there is vulnerability, truth, and accountability.

Most churches can create a network of discipleship covenant groups of three to five people. Some call these micro groups. Well-oriented mature Christians (deacons, altar workers, etc.) can be the first group of potential disciple makers. According to Ogden, the disciple maker has the following duties: keeper of the covenant within the group (to grow together, be transparent, keep confidence, be accountable, etc.), give invitation to accountable relationships, be the group convener and guide, prepare curriculum-based lessons and outcome-considered assignments, and model transparency.

There is good news in George Barna's recent study on why believers are not discipling others for churches wishing to adopt a new paradigm of ministry focused on disciple making. Thirty-seven percent of respondents in this study reported they are not discipling another person because they don't think they are qualified or equipped. Twenty-four percent chose the answer "no one has suggested it/asked me," and 22 percent just haven't thought about it.[68] This survey should encourage pastors and church leaders to seize the moment. What a time to begin equipping the believers! What a time to remind them of the priority of the Great Commission! What a great occasion to make church members think about discipleship and disciple making!

Most books on discipleship are prescriptive. I am intentionally trying to be descriptive instead so every congregation can develop a unique program that makes sense in their context. I have presented information on both the theory and practice of discipleship and spiritual formation to make this possible. To me, it is more important to make sure all the elements of discipling and disciple making are included in a program than insist on having a particular form or format in all congregations.

A successful ministry of disciple making in local churches requires personal sacrifices and the investment of life and money on the part of everyone involved. A flexible approach to any program is the key to its success. This chapter contains essential information to help any church to begin the process of becoming a disciple-making church. Every member becoming a disciple, experiencing true spiritual transformation, and becoming a disciple maker is the goal. True disciples of Jesus can turn the world "upside down" (Acts 17:6). Once initiated, this effort remains a continuing ministry of the church, paving the way for all believers to go from membership to discipleship, learning, growing, forming, serving, and living as citizens of the kingdom of God. Properly and prayerfully designed and initiated, this effort can make the true mission of the church—the Great Commission—the implemented mission of every church.

www.thomsonkmathew.com

NOTES

1 "Excerpt: A Rapid Decline in Pastoral Security," Barna, March 15, 2023, https://www.barna.com/research/pastoral-security-confidence.
2 See Ed Stetzer, *Christians in the Age of Outrage: How to Bring Our Best When the World Is at Its Worst* (Carol Stream, IL: Tyndale, 2018).
3 George Barna, *The State of Discipleship* (Ventura, CA: Barna Group, 2015), 36.
4 Greg Ogden, *Transforming Discipleship: Making Disciples a Few at a Time* (Downers Grove, IL: Intervarsity, 2016), 27.
5 George Barna, *Maximum Faith: Live Like Jesus* (Ventura, CA: Metaformation, 2011), 29.
6 The startling results of the Willow Creek study titled *Reveal* were published by the church in 2007.
7 Barna Group, "New Research on the State of Discipleship," Leadership, December 1, 2015, www.barna.com/research/new-research-on-the-state-of-discipleship, accessed April 8, 2024.
8 Data based on Pew Research Center, "Religious 'Nones' in America: Who They Are and What They Believe," Pew Research Center Report, January 24, 2024, https://www.pewresearch.org/religion/2024/01/24/religious-nones-in-america-who-they-are-and-what-they-believe/.
9 Ogden, *Transforming Discipleship*, 24.
10 Juan Carlos Ortiz, *Disciple* (Carol Stream, IL: Creation House, 1975), 60–64.

11 Leroy Eims, *The Lost Art of Disciple Making* (Grand Rapids, MI: Zondervan, 1978), 59–61.

12 Kent Carlson and Mike Lueken, *Renovation of the Church: What Happens When a Seeker Church Discovers Spiritual Formation* (Downers Grove, IL: Intervarsity, 2011), 33–35.

13 Ogden, *Transforming Discipleship*, 52.

14 See Ogden, *Transforming Discipleship*, 54.

15 See Ogden, *Transforming Discipleship*, 62.

16 A. W. Tozer, *Discipleship: What It Truly Means to Be a Christian: Collected Insights from A. W. Tozer* (Chicago: Moody, 2018), 12.

17 Tozer, *Discipleship*, 47.

18 Tozer, *Discipleship*, 78.

19 Dietrich Bonhoeffer, *The Cost of Discipleship*, trans. R. H. Fuller and Irmgard Booth, rev. ed. (New York: Macmillan, 1963), 97.

20 Bobby Harrington and Josh Patrick, *The Disciple-Maker's Handbook: 7 Elements of a Discipleship Lifestyle* (New York: HarperCollins, 2017), 35.

21 Harrington and Patrick, T*he Disciple-Maker's Handbook,* 46–60.

22 Harrington and Patrick, *The Disciple-Maker's Handbook*, 111.

23 See Harrington and Patrick, *The Disciple-Maker's Handbook*, 166.

24 Jonathan K. Dodson, *Gospel-Centered Discipleship* (Wheaton, IL: Crossway, 2012), 35.

25 Dodson, *Gospel-Centered Discipleship*, 46.

26 James W. Fowler, *Stages of Faith: The Psychology of Human Development and the Quest for Meaning* (New York: Harper Collins, 1981).

27 Erik H. Erikson, *Childhood and Society* (New York: Norton, 1987).

28 Leroy Aden, David G. Benner, and J. Harold Ellens, eds., *Christian Perspectives on Human Development* (Grand Rapids, MI: Baker, 1992).

29 John H. Westerhoff, *Will Our Children Have Faith?* (New York: Seabury, 1976).

30 Peter L. Scazzero, *The Emotionally Healthy Church: A Strategy for Discipleship That Actually Changes Lives*, updated and expanded ed. (Grand Rapids, MI: Zondervan, 2010), 10.

31 Scazzero, *The Emotionally Healthy Church*, 214.

32 Paul W. Pruyser, *The Minister as Diagnostician: Personal Problems in Pastoral Perspective* (Philadelphia: Westminster, 1976).

33 Henri J. M. Nouwen, *Spiritual Formation: Following the Movement of the Spirit* (New York: HarperOne, 2010).

34 Nouwen, *Spiritual Formation*, xvi.

35 Nouwen, *Spiritual Formation*, 5.

36 Nouwen, *Spiritual Formation*, 55.

37 Alan Andrews, ed., *The Kingdom Life: A Practical Theology of Discipleship and Spiritual Formation* (Colorado Springs: NavPress, 2010). See also Dallas Willard, *The Spirit of the Disciplines: Understanding How God Changes Lives* (San Francisco: HarperSanFrancisco, 1990).

38 See the first volume in this series, J. W. Phillips, *Pursuing a Divine Life: A Study of the New Nature*, The Pursuing with Passion Series (Honolulu, HI: HCC, 2013).

39 H. Richard Niebuhr, *The Purpose of the Church and Its Ministry* (New York: Harper & Row, 1956), 64.

40 The following section is indebted to Thomson K. Mathew, *Spirit-Led Ministry in the 21st Century*, rev. and updated ed. (Bloomington, IN: Westbow, 2017).

41 David W. Bennett, *Metaphors of Ministry: Biblical Images of Leaders and Followers* (Grand Rapids, MI: Baker, 1993), 53–54.

42 Dietrich Bonhoeffer, *Creation and Fall Temptation: Two Biblical Studies* (1959; repr., New York: Touchstone, 1997), 95.

43 George A. Buttrick, *God, Pain and Evil* (Nashville: Abingdon, 1966), 55.

44 E. Stanley Jones, *Christ and Human Suffering* (New York: Abingdon, 1933).

45 C. S. Lewis, *The Problem of Pain* (New York: Macmillan, 1962), 93.

46 Thomson K. Mathew, "The Grace Revolution and Person-Centered Therapy: A Comparative Analysis from a Pastoral Care Perspective" in *The Truth About Grace: Spirit-Empowered Perspectives*, ed. Vinson Synan (Lake Mary, FL: Charisma House, 2018), 58–70.

47 Donald E. Messer, *Contemporary Images of Christian Ministry* (Nashville: Abingdon, 1989).

48 William H. Willimon, *Pastor: The Theology and Practice of Ordained Ministry* (Nashville: Abingdon, 2000).

49 John W. Frye, *Jesus the Pastor: Leading Others in the Character and Power of Christ* (Grand Rapids, MI: Zondervan, 2000), 50–54.

50 William A. Clebsch and Charles R. Jaekle, *Pastoral Care in Historical Perspective* (Englewood Cliffs: Prentice Hall, 1963).

51 Henri J. M. Nouwen, *Creative Ministry* (Garden City, NY: Image, 1971), 110.

52 Earl E. Shelp and Ronald Sunderland, eds., *A Biblical Basis for Ministry* (Philadelphia: Westminster, 1981), 136.

53 Frank Newport, "In U.S., 77% Identify as Christian," Gallup News, December 24, 2012, http://news.gallup.com/poll/159548/identify-christian.aspx; Ed Stetzer, "Too Many So-Called Christians Merely Giving Lip Service to Jesus," Charisma News, March 28, 2014, https://www.charismanews.com/opinion/43298-christian-it-s-more-than-just-a-label; Kelly Shattuck, "7 Startling Facts: An Up Close Look at Church Attendance in America," *Church Leaders*, December 14, 2017, https://churchleaders.com/pastors/pastor-articles/139575-7-startling-facts-an-up-close-look-at-church-attendance-in-america.html.

54 Lawrence Richards, *You, the Teacher* (Chicago: Moody Press, 1972), 66–67.

55 Ronald G. Held, *Learning Together* (Springfield, MO: Gospel Publishing House, 1976), 34.

56 Leonard Sweet, *Post-Modern Pilgrims: First Century Passion for the 21st Century World* (Nashville: Broadman & Holman, 2000).

57 Malcolm S. Knowles, *Self-Directed Learning: A Guide for Learners and Teachers* (Chicago: Association Press, 1975), 19.

58 Knowles, *Self-Directed Learning*, 59–63.

59 Benjamin Bloom, *Taxonomy of Educational Objectives* (New York: Longman, Green, and Co., 1956).

60 Raymond Wlodkowski, *Enhancing Adult Motivation to Learn: A Guide to Improving Instruction and Increasing Learner Achievement* (San Francisco: Jossey-Bass, 1988).

61 Richard Paul and Linda Elder, *A Miniature Guide for Those Who Teach on How to Improve Student Learning* (Dillon Beach, CA: Foundation for Critical Thinking, 2002).

62 Charles V. Gerkin, *An Introduction to Pastoral Care* (Nashville: Abingdon, 1997).

63 Scazzero, *The Emotionally Healthy Church*, 211.

64 Scazzero, *The Emotionally Healthy Church*, 223–25.

65 Scazzero, *The Emotionally Healthy Church*, 218.

66 Harrington and Patrick, *The Disciple-Maker's Handbook.*

67 Francis Chan, *Multiply: Disciples Making Disciples* (Colorado Springs: David C. Cook, 2012).

68 "New Research on the State of Discipleship," Barna, December 1, 2015, www.barna.com/research/new-research-on-the-state-of-discipleship. See also, "Two in Five Christians Are Not Engaged in Discipleship," Barna, January 26, 2022, https://www.barna.com/research/christians-discipleship-community.

BIBLIOGRAPHY

Aden, LeRoy, David G. Benner, and J. Harold Ellens, eds. *Christian Perspectives on Human Development.* Grand Rapids, MI: Baker, 1992.

Andrews, Alan, ed. *The Kingdom Life: A Practical Theology of Discipleship and Spiritual Formation.* Colorado Springs: NavPress, 2010.

Barna, George. *Maximum Faith: Live Like Jesus.* Ventura, CA: Metaformation, 2011.

Bennett, David W. *Metaphors of Ministry: Biblical Images of Leaders and Followers.* Grand Rapids, MI: Baker, 1993.

Bloesch, Donald. *Jesus Christ: Savior and Lord.* Downers Grove, IL: InterVarsity, 1997.

Bonhoeffer, Dietrich. *The Cost of Discipleship.* Translated by R. H. Fuller and Irmgard Booth. Revised edition. New York: Macmillan, 1963.

Brother Lawrence. *The Practice of the Presence of God.* Grand Rapids, MI: Spire, 1958.

Carlson, Kent, and Mike Lueken. *Renovation of the Church: What Happens When a Seeker Church Discovers Spiritual Formation.* Downers Grove, IL: InterVarsity, 2011.

Chan, Francis. *Multiply: Disciples Making Disciples.* Colorado Springs: David C. Cook, 2012.

Chandler, Diane J. *Christian Spiritual Formation: An Integrated Approach for Personal and Relational Wholeness.* Downers Grove, IL: InterVarsity, 2014.

Clebsch, William A., and Charles R. Jaekle. *Pastoral Care in Historical Perspective*. Englewood Cliffs, NJ: Prentice Hall, 1963.

Dodson, Jonathan K. *Gospel-Centered Discipleship*. Wheaton, IL: Crossway, 2012.

Erikson, Erik H. *Childhood and Society*. New York: Norton, 1987.

Foster, Richard. *Celebration of Discipline: The Path to Spiritual Growth*. San Francisco: HarperSanFrancisco, 1998.

Fowler, James W. *Stages of Faith: The Psychology of Human Development and the Quest for Meaning*. New York: Harper Collins, 1981.

Frye, John W. *Jesus the Pastor: Leading Others in the Character and Power of Christ*. Grand Rapids, MI: Zondervan, 2000.

Gangel, Kenneth O., and James C. Wilhoit, eds. *The Christian Educator's Handbook on Spiritual Formation*. Wheaton: Victor, 1994.

Gerkin, Charles V. *An Introduction to Pastoral Care*. Nashville: Abingdon, 1997.

Harrington, Bobby, and Josh Patrick. *The Disciple Maker's Handbook: 7 Elements of a Discipleship Lifestyle*. New York: HarperCollins, 2017.

Held, Ronald G. *Learning Together*. Springfield, MO: Gospel Publishing House, 1976.

Henrichsen, Walter A. *Disciples Are Made Not Born: Helping Others Grow to Maturity in Christ*. Colorado Springs: David C. Cook, 1988.

Hull, Bill. *The Disciple Making Pastor*. Old Tappan, NJ: Revell, 1988.

Jones, E. Stanley. *Christ and Human Suffering*. New York: Abingdon, 1933.

Knowles, Malcolm S. *Self-Directed Learning: A Guide for Learners and Teachers*. Chicago: Association Press, 1975.

Lewis, C. S. *The Problem of Pain*. New York: Macmillan, 1962.

Mathew, Thomson K. *Spirit-Led Ministry in the 21st Century*. Revised and updated edition. Bloomington, IN: Westbow, 2017.

Mathew, Thomson K. *Spiritual Identity and Spirit-Empowered Life*. Kottayam, Kerala, India: Goodnews Books, 2017.

Mathew, Thomson K. *What Will Your Tombstone Say? 52 Short Essays on Spirit-Filled Church, Spirit-Led Ministry, and Spirit-Empowered Discipleship*. North Charleston, SC: Createspace, 2018.

Messer, Donald E. *Contemporary Images of Christian Ministry*. Nashville: Abingdon, 1989.

Mulholland, M. Robert. *Invitation to a Journey: A Roadmap for Spiritual Formation*. Downers Grove, IL: InterVarsity, 2016.

Niebuhr, H. Richard, and Daniel D. Williams, eds. *The Ministry in Historical Perspective*. San Francisco: Harper & Row, 1983.

Nouwen, Henri J. M. *Creative Ministry*. Garden City, NY: Image, 1971.

Nouwen, Henri J. M. *Spiritual Formation: Following the Movement of the Spirit*. New York: HarperOne, 2010.

Ogden, Greg. *Discipleship Essentials: A Guide to Building Your Life in Christ*. Downers Grove, IL: InterVarsity, 2007.

Ogden, Greg. *Transforming Discipleship: Making Disciples a Few at a Time*. Downers Grove, IL: InterVarsity, 2016.

Ortiz, Juan Carlos. *Disciple*. Carol Stream, IL: Creation House, 1975.

Peterson, Eugene H. *Working the Angles: The Shape of Pastoral Integrity*. Grand Rapids, MI: Eerdmans, 1987.

Phillips, J. W. *Pursuing a Divine Life: A Study of the New Nature*. The Pursuing with Passion Series. Honolulu, HI: HCC, 2013.

Platt, David. *Follow Me: A Call to Die, A Call to Live*. Carol Stream, IL: Tyndale, 2013.

Pruyser, Paul W. *The Minister as Diagnostician: Personal Problems in Pastoral Perspective*. Philadelphia: Westminster, 1976.

Richard, Paul, and Linda Elder. *A Miniature Guide for Those Who Teach on How to Improve Student Learning*. Dillon Beach, CA: Foundation for Critical Thinking, 2002.

Scazzero, Peter L. *The Emotionally Healthy Church: A Strategy for Discipleship That Actually Changes Lives.* Updated and expanded edition. Grand Rapids, MI: Zondervan, 2010.

Scazzero, Peter L. *Emotionally Healthy Spirituality: It's Impossible to Be Spiritually Mature, While Remaining Emotionally Immature*. Grand Rapids, MI: Zondervan, 2017.

Shelp, Earl E., and Ronald Sunderland, eds. *A Biblical Basis for Ministry*. Philadelphia: Westminster, 1981.

Sweet, Leonard. *Post-Modern Pilgrims: First Century Passion for the 21st Century World.* Nashville: Broadman & Holman, 2000.

Synan, Vinson, ed. *The Truth About Grace: Spirit-Empowered Perspectives.* Lake Mary, FL: Charisma House, 2018.

Taylor, Richard S. *The Disciplined Life: The Mark of Christian Maturity*. Minneapolis: Bethany, 2002.

Thomas à Kempis. *The Imitation of Christ.* London: Penguin, 1952.

Tozer, A. W. *Discipleship: What It Truly Means to Be a Christian: Collected Insights from A. W. Tozer*. Chicago: Moody, 2018.

Westerhoff, John H. *Will Our Children Have Faith?* New York: Seabury, 1976.

Whitney, Donald S. *Spiritual Disciplines for the Christian Life*. Colorado Springs: NavPress, 2002.

Willard, Dallas. *The Spirit of the Disciplines: Understanding How God Changes Lives.* San Francisco: HarperSanFrancisco, 1990.

Willimon, William H. *Pastor: The Theology and Practice of Ordained Ministry*. Nashville: Abingdon, 2000.

Wlodkowski, Raymond J. *Enhancing Adult Motivation to Learn: A Guide to Improving Instruction and Increasing Learner Achievement.* San Francisco: Jossey-Bass, 1988.